PIANO AND KEYBOARD MASTERY

A Complete Guide with Theory and Exercises for All Skill Levels

MUSIC MASTERY SERIES, VOLUME 3

By Tad Sisler

For my loving mother Elaine, who sacrificed her career as an internationally renowned classical pianist to raise her family, instilling in me a deep love for the piano from a very early age.

TABLE OF CONTENTS: PAGE

FOREWORD

I had a head-start in learning to love how to play the piano. My mother, **Elaine Witt Sisler**, was a child prodigy. Her mother took her to a yard sale when she was three, and a piano was sitting on the house's front lawn. My mother immediately went up to the piano and started playing, as if she was remembering from another lifetime. By the age of five, my mother was giving recitals. At 17, she was a famous pianist and featured piano soloist with the **Chicago Symphony** during the height of World War II. When my father returned from three years in the Navy in the South Pacific, they married, and she became a mother and a housewife.

Tad Sisler's Mother, Elaine Witt Sisler at Age 16
Source – Sisler Private Collection

When I was growing up, my mother taught piano lessons in our house, primarily to children. Her patience was incredible to me, knowing how gifted she was. On occasion, my parents would have small house parties at night. She would play *Chopin's E-Minor Concerto* or *Clair De Lune,* and I would sit at the top of the stairs out of sight, marveling at her perfection as a pianist.

She started teaching me the fundamentals of piano as soon as I could walk. Playing the piano is in my DNA. I had a great-grandparent who also was a concert pianist. I'm unsure how genetics figures into anyone's decision to learn the piano. I know many people with no history of musicians in their families who became great on their own, but it all starts with the desire. Like anything, you must want it, and you can't be forced into it by someone who wants it for you if you don't like it yourself.

Nothing is more rewarding than sitting down and playing a song on the piano. No matter what kind of stress you may be under, it goes away immediately when you play.

As I improved my skills, I became more satisfied and enthusiastic, wanting to learn not just the classical pieces my teachers put in front of me but also my favorite songs across different genres. My ear training became more sophisticated as time passed, and my confidence to perform in front of others went through the roof.

Most people doubt or wonder if they have the ability or talent to learn an instrument. There are always concerns about not having enough time to practice regularly. Can you afford the instrument? (Hint: You can start learning on a dirt-cheap used keyboard or rent a piano at a meager monthly payment.) Maybe they failed to learn an instrument previously and are skeptical about trying again. Others want to know their favorite music to play and don't want to be bothered with other genres.

From my own experience, I became proficient in playing step by step and learned music theory naturally along the way because I enjoyed the learning process. My goal in this book is to help the reader engage in an enjoyable learning experience that keeps them motivated and excited about practicing. Loving what you do is the key to happiness!

In sixth grade, I took an advanced typing course and quickly learned how to type 80 words per minute. Little did I know then that later in life, the two most important skills I would need when producing digital music were mastery of the computer keyboard and the piano-style keyboard, the main instrument used with computer interfaces to program and record music.

"When I had nothing else, I had my mother and the piano. And you know what? They were all I needed." – Alicia Keys

Alicia Keys
Credit – Creativecommons.org

When I was around twelve, my mother felt she couldn't teach me more. She put me with her friend, the internationally renowned classical pianist **Joanna Hodges**. I would go to practice rooms at the local college three or four days a week and learn complicated classical pieces, with Joanna hovering over me, showing me what goes beyond technique itself.

She emphasized emotional performance, highlighting crescendos and decrescendos, and she was a perfectionist. Soon, I was winning superior ratings in performance competitions.

Joanna Hodges
Source – Joanna Hodges

Then, a significant change occurred. My parents' divorce led to a relocation, 2000 miles away, to a small farm town in Missouri with my father. He, aware of my love for the piano, brought an old out-of-tune upright piano into our home. Throughout my teenage years, I eagerly returned from school to play every popular song I knew by ear, often forgetting the classical pieces. The foundation was already there, and I found joy in entertaining my high school friends with my piano skills. I also was fortunate to be the only student in the lower quarter of Southern Missouri to make *All-State Choir*. Other guys lettered in football. I lettered in choir. Not completely macho, I guess, but that's where all the pretty girls were!

My career path took a significant turn during my Junior year in High School when I attended a **Billy Joel** concert. His youthful energy and stage presence, observed from a close distance, inspired me to pursue a full-time career in music.

I spent my life performing, even while raising my children, and have played thousands of gigs across various genres over a 40-year period.

In the early 2000s, I was hired as a developer for pianos and keyboards by **Yamaha Corporation of America**, and for ten years, I learned from the finest developers exactly how to program music on the highest levels, manipulating midi files to breathe as if they were being performed live by the best performer, dissecting popular songs and separating instruments by ear from recordings, then reproducing the sounds and notes to sound as close to the original recordings as possible. It was a great learning experience, and it led me to the point where I produced hundreds of my compositions and other music in recording studios, composed soundtracks for feature films and documentaries, and performed with the industry giants.

I'm a voting member of the **Academy of Recording Arts & Sciences**, helping to choose **Grammy** winners each year. In 2023, I won a **Telly Award**. As an author, I recently won a coveted **Reader's Favorite Award** for a biography I wrote on the life of a famous trumpeter. I'm grateful to do my best to impart the wisdom and knowledge I've gained through extensive experience to help you become a great pianist and keyboardist, no matter where you are in your skills.

INTRODUCTION

I designed this book so that students can learn from the ground up and for teachers to use it as a road map for their students. Let's begin with two compelling stories about two great pianists who lived and performed centuries apart.

COMPOSER SPOTLIGHT
LUDWIG VAN BEETHOVEN

One of the most revered composers and pianists in classical music history, **Ludwig van Beethoven** had an extraordinary journey from a young prodigy to an icon whose works continue to inspire generations.

Beethoven was born in Bonn, Germany, in 1770. His father, **Johann van Beethoven**, recognized **Ludwig's** amazing musical talent early on. He pushed him into rigorous training, hoping to create a child prodigy like **Mozart**. Despite his father's harsh and demanding practices, **Beethoven's** passion for music grew. The passion for music was in his blood.

At 17, **Beethoven** moved to Vienna, the musical capital of Europe at the time, to study with **Joseph Haydn**. He struggled financially in Vienna, but his determination and dedication to music were unwavering. Beethoven spent countless hours practicing piano, composing, and immersing himself in the vibrant music of his era. Beethoven's emotional depth and bold innovations showed that he was already developing his own style in his early compositions. His piano sonatas and symphonies broke the conventional rules of classical music, introducing new structures and expressions. Despite facing profound deafness in his late 20s, Beethoven's creativity and genius flourished. He composed some of his greatest "works, including the *"Moonlight Sonata, "Fifth Symphony," and "Ninth Symphony,"* redefining the possibilities of music.

Towards the end of his life, Beethoven lost his hearing. I read a story once about **Beethoven**, almost entirely deaf, performing his *Ninth Symphony* with an orchestra in front of a live audience for the first time. When he finished, he started crying, not hearing any applause, because he thought the audience hated it. Then, the concertmaster went to the piano and gently turned **Beethoven** towards the audience. To his astonishment, they were giving him a thundering standing ovation, cheering at the beauty of the composition they had just experienced.

Ludwig Van Beethoven
Credit – Wikipedia

Beethoven's journey from a young, ambitious pianist to a legendary composer and performer is an excellent example of extraordinary resilience, persistence against all odds, and dedication to your craft. He transcended personal adversity and revolutionized classical music.

ARTIST SPOTLIGHT
ELTON JOHN

Elton John
Credit – Creativecommons.org

It's almost silly to me to put **Elton John** into the same conversation with **Beethoven**. Their styles are as far apart as one could imagine, but their journeys were both extraordinary examples of wild success in different eras. In fact, **Elton John** had a string of *Top Ten Hits* each year for 25 years in a row, and he charted songs in five different decades. When I was twelve, my older sister took me to see a young **Elton John performing** at the San Diego, California *Sports Arena*. I was transfixed, and I was also one of the very few people in that audience who witnessed **Elton** perform again more than fifty years later at *Petco Park* in San Diego. He still sounded great fifty years later, although he strolled to the stage at *Petco*, instead of jumping all over the place as he had done when I was a boy.

Elton John has a compelling story that illustrates his journey from a young pianist to a global superstar. His path to fame was marked by determination, resilience, and unyielding passion for music. Like **Beethoven** (and me), the love of music was in his blood.

Born as **Reginald Kenneth Dwight** on March 25, 1947, in Pinner, England, **Elton John** showed musical talent at an early age. By age three, he could play *"The Skater's Waltz"* by ear. His grandmother was a big influence, encouraging his interest in music and introducing him to the piano.

He had formal piano lessons by age seven, and his talent quickly became apparent.

At 11, **Elton** won a scholarship to the **Royal Academy of Music in** London, where he studied for several years. Again, like me, despite his classical training, he was drawn to rock and roll. **Elton** was influenced by artists like **Elvis Presley** and **Little Richard**. As a teenager, he joined his first band, **Bluesology,** playing local gigs and backing American R&B acts touring the UK.

In the late 1960s, **Elton** met lyricist **Bernie Taupin** through a chance encounter. This partnership would become one of the most successful in music history. Initially, they needed help to make a breakthrough. Still, their persistence paid off with the release of **Elton's** self-titled album in 1970, which included the hit single *"Your Song."* This song marked the beginning of his rise to stardom.

The 1970s were a golden era for **Elton John**. Albums like *"Goodbye Yellow Brick Road," "Honky Chateau," and "Captain Fantastic and the Brown Dirt Cowboy"* became massive hits. His live performances were legendary, characterized by his flamboyant costumes and energetic stage presence. **Elton's** ability to blend rock, pop, and classical influences set him apart from his contemporaries.

Elton John battled substance abuse, depression, and personal struggles, taking a toll on his health and career.
By the late 1980s, he sought help and successfully overcame his addictions, marking a new chapter in his life and career.

Today, **Elton John** is celebrated not only for his musical achievements but also for his contributions to society. **Elton** continues to inspire fans around the world.

TRANSFORM YOURSELF

My book aims to guide readers through a transformative musical journey, much like the paths of legendary pianists like **Ludwig van Beethoven** and **Elton John**. By emphasizing the mastery of techniques, understanding of music theory, and the joy of learning, this book provides a comprehensive roadmap for aspiring musicians. Drawing inspiration from **Beethoven's** resilience in the face of adversity and **Elton John's** evolution from a young prodigy to a global superstar (along with many other examples through the book), I hope you'll find motivation and practical guidance at every stage of your development.

Beethoven's dedication to mastering complex techniques despite his profound deafness and **Elton John's** innovative blend of classical and rock influences highlight the importance of a solid technical foundation and an appreciation for music theory. I designed this book to make these foundational skills accessible and engaging, ensuring that readers develop proficiency and cultivate a lifelong love for playing. By incorporating exercises, real-life stories, and motivational tips, this book encourages readers to enjoy the process, embrace challenges, and ultimately achieve their musical goals.

SELF-DISCIPLINE

Many people have told me, *"I always wanted to learn how to play piano, but I have no self-discipline."* Self-discipline is not something you have or don't have. It's something you make happen. Whether you're a religious person or not, you can understand the concept that when God created us, we were given this amazing power to choose, a power so strong that we actually can use it to choose against God if we want to. I understand the power of addictions, but we can choose to overcome smoking or drugs, or anything we put our minds to. Self-discipline is your choice. You can become the best at what you do if you decide that there is no other option but success. This all starts with self-discipline, with your choice to make it happen, and then to persist until you've succeeded. It's that simple. If you don't believe you can learn an instrument, you probably won't. But I promise you, if you follow the wisdom and resources of this book, you will find your way if you stick with it.

I meticulously designed the structure of this book to cater to musicians at every stage of your learning journey. Organized into clear, progressive chapters, I begin with foundational basics and gradually advance to more complex techniques, ensuring that each concept builds upon the previous one.

This step-by-step approach allows you to develop your skills systematically, making the learning process manageable and effective. I've structured each chapter with practical exercises and a concluding segue to the next topic, fostering a seamless learning experience. I include case studies, anecdotes, and real-life stories, providing relatable and motivational context to the technical instructions.

I want you to persevere and enjoy your musical journey. Drawing on the inspirational stories of great performers through the ages, I emphasize the joy and fulfillment of mastering your instrument, addressing common challenges. This book offers practical tips for overcoming them, hopefully instilling a sense of confidence and excitement in you. Throughout the book, I remind you to embrace the process and celebrate your progress.

Through your journey, I strongly encourage you to believe in yourself. Understand that everyone encounters the exact obstacles you do. I assure you that many people who have lesser talent than others become very successful at their craft. You have a unique magic within yourself. You also have the power to turn frustration in any moment into the realization that you are in the process of learning something you will get endless enjoyment from doing.

Let me paraphrase a quote from Elvis Costello:

"I used to get angry, now I get amused!"

Remember that as you work your way through the hard parts, mastering music is one of life's most rewarding things.

Medical Disclaimer:

The information provided in this book is intended for informational and educational purposes only and should not be used as a substitute for professional medical advice, diagnosis, or treatment. Always seek the advice of your physician or a qualified healthcare provider with any questions you may have regarding a medical condition or before beginning any new health, fitness, exercise, breathing, or dietary regimen.

The exercises, techniques, and suggestions in this book may not be suitable for everyone and could result in injury or adverse effects. If you have an existing health condition or suspect you may have one, consult a licensed medical professional before attempting any of the practices outlined herein.

The author and publisher explicitly disclaim any responsibility for any adverse effects, injuries, or damages that may result from the use or misuse of the information presented in this book.

Legal Disclaimer:

The author and publisher have made every effort to ensure the accuracy and reliability of the information contained in this book at the time of publication. However, errors, omissions, or inaccuracies may occur. The author and publisher make no guarantees regarding the completeness, reliability, or applicability of the information provided. They explicitly disclaim any liability for any loss, damage, or disruption caused by errors, omissions, or actions taken based on the content of this book, regardless of the cause, including negligence or accident.

The content in this book is provided for general informational purposes only and does not constitute professional advice of any kind, including medical, legal, or financial advice. If you require specific guidance, please consult a qualified professional in the relevant field.

The author and publisher make no guarantees or promises regarding the effectiveness, results, or outcomes of any techniques, strategies, or recommendations presented in this book. Readers are responsible for using their own judgment and discretion when applying the material in their personal or professional lives.

Further, any external quotes, references, online courses, books, or products mentioned in this book are for informational purposes only and do not imply endorsement, approval, or promotion by the author or publisher. The inclusion of such material does not constitute a guarantee of quality or effectiveness.

CHAPTER ONE
GETTING STARTED WITH PIANO AND KEYBOARDS

It is surprising and somewhat disheartening that approximately ninety percent of students who start learning an instrument quit within the first year. It's like joining the gym in January as a New Year's resolution, and then promptly quitting when you get tired. Experts attribute this high dropout rate to various factors such as lack of motivation, insufficient practice, unrealistic expectations, and inadequate support. Many beginners need help with the initial learning curve, facing challenges that can feel insurmountable without proper guidance and encouragement. This statistic underscores the importance of a well-structured, engaging, and supportive learning environment to help new musicians overcome early obstacles and stay committed to their musical journey.

On the flip side, the potential for success is immense for those who persist. Research shows that individuals who continue practicing an instrument beyond the initial year often excel and achieve a high level of proficiency. With consistent practice and dedication, around eighty percent of long-term learners report significant improvement in their playing skills and overall musicality. These individuals not only master their instruments but also enjoy numerous cognitive, emotional, and social benefits. This contrast underscores the transformative power of perseverance and the profound rewards that come from sustained effort in learning an instrument. By sticking with the process, you can unlock your full potential and experience the joy and fulfillment that music brings.

What does this mean for you? **Believe in yourself** and understand that nothing is easy initially. In that case, you have a solid chance of becoming great at this. Just stick with it. You may lack coordination, but it's all about repetition. Please do it again until it starts to feel comfortable. If you begin to get frustrated, let it be the fuel that fires your passion to get through it. From personal experience, I can tell you that it gets good quickly when you become even slightly proficient.

"There's nothing remarkable about it. All one has to do is hit the right keys at the right time and the instrument plays itself."
– Johann Sebastian Bach

Johann Sebastian Bach
Source — Wikipedia

THE ORIGIN OF THE PIANO

The piano originated in the early 18th century. Its invention is attributed to an Italian instrument maker, **Bartolomeo Cristofori**, who worked for the **Medici** family in Florence. **Cristofori's** creation, initially called the "gravicembalo col piano e forte" (harpsichord with soft and loud), was designed to address the limitations of the harpsichord and clavichord, two popular keyboard instruments of the time. Cristofori's piano utilized a hammer mechanism that allowed players to vary the volume of each note based on the force with which someone struck the keys. This innovation marked a significant advancement in musical expression and dynamics.

INSTRUMENTS THAT PRECEDED THE PIANO

Before the piano, other keyboard instruments laid the groundwork for its development. The harpsichord, prominent from the 16th to the 18th centuries, produced sound by plucking strings with quills when keys were pressed. While it allowed for intricate and rapid playing, it lacked dynamic range, meaning all notes were played at the same volume (in the early days of computer music programming, we came across the same obstacle). The clavichord, another predecessor, used a tangent to strike the strings, allowing for some dynamic control and vibrato, but its sound was relatively quiet, making it unsuitable for large performances. The organ provided greater volume and sustained notes with its pipes and bellows. Still, it was limited in dynamic expression and tactile response.

Since the advent of the early great composers, many iconic pianists interpreted their work with depth and passion, including **Martha Argerich**, widely considered to be one of the greatest pianists of all time. She is technically brilliant, her interpretations are passionate, and she is considered a leading figure in classical music since the 1960s. Study and enjoy her uplifting performances.

Martha Argerich
Credit – Romina Santarelli – Wikimedia Commons

EVOLUTION AND ADOPTION OF THE PIANO

Cristofori's early pianos, though revolutionary, underwent further development and refinement throughout the 18th and 19th centuries. Innovations such as adding an escapement mechanism, allowing the hammer to fall away from the string after striking it, and improvements in string tension and soundboard construction contributed to the piano's enhanced sound quality and playability. By the late 18th century, composers like **Wolfgang Amadeus Mozart** began composing specifically for the piano, recognizing its expressive potential. The 19th century saw the instrument's full adoption and popularity, with composers such as **Ludwig van Beethoven** and **Frédéric Chopin** writing extensively for the piano, exploiting its dynamic range and expressive capabilities. Conveying emotions and dynamics solidified the piano's place in solo and ensemble settings, leading to its enduring presence in music.

SECTION ONE
CHOOSING THE RIGHT INSTRUMENT

TYPES OF PIANOS AND KEYBOARDS

ACOUSTIC PIANOS, either upright or grand piano style, are traditional pianos that produce sound through the mechanical action of hammers striking strings. Grand pianos have a horizontal frame and strings, with a rich, resonant sound ideal for concert performances. Upright pianos, with vertical frames and strings, are more compact and suited for home use.

Advantages: Rich, authentic sound; dynamic range; responsive touch.

Disadvantages: It requires regular tuning and maintenance; it is large, heavy, and expensive.

DIGITAL PIANOS use electronic sound synthesis to replicate the sound and feel of an acoustic piano. They often include volume control, headphone jacks, and built-in recording capabilities. Digital pianos can range from compact, portable models to full-sized instruments with weighted keys. Digital pianos sounded synthy and clunky until the mid-1990s with the advent of the **Kurzweil** digital pianos. Since then, most brands' sound quality has become outstanding, and touch sensitivity has become excellent.

Advantages: No tuning is required, volume control is portable, and it is often more affordable.

Disadvantages: Acoustic pianos may be more authentic in sound and touch.

KEYBOARDS are versatile, portable instruments with many sounds and features, used in contemporary music settings and including a wide range of tones, from piano to synthesizer sounds. Keyboards typically have lighter keys and can be used for performance and music production.

The three most popular sizes of keyboards are 61-key, 76-key, and 88-key keyboards. When learning to play using a keyboard, you should get the 88-key keyboards if you can. Keyboards generally are grouped into "organ style" with non-weighted keys and "piano style" with weighted keys. Weighted key models most resemble the piano itself. I advise that you learn with weighted keys if available to you.

Advantages: Lightweight and portable; wide range of sounds and features; affordable.

Disadvantages: Lighter keys may not replicate the feel of a piano; sound quality varies.

SYNTHESIZERS are electronic instruments designed to generate various sounds. They are often used in music production and performance. Synths allow you to create and manipulate sounds through multiple methods, such as subtractive synthesis, FM synthesis, and sampling. Synthesizers can be standalone or integrated into keyboards.

Advantages: Highly versatile sound creation; essential for electronic music; extensive sound manipulation capabilities.

Disadvantages: Learning can be complex and requires external amplification for live performance.

HYBRID PIANOS combine the mechanical action of acoustic pianos with digital sound technology. They offer the feel and response of an acoustic piano while providing the benefits of digital features, such as headphone jacks, recording options, and various sound settings.

Advantages: Combines the best of acoustic and digital pianos; authentic touch and sound; additional digital features.

Disadvantages: More expensive than standard digital pianos; still requires some maintenance.

Truly, there is no perfect substitute for a high-quality tuned grand piano. Where to begin? Here are some critical considerations for beginners:

BUDGET: Determine how much you will spend on your first instrument. Acoustic pianos can be expensive, ranging from $3,000 to $50,000. Digital pianos and keyboards are generally more affordable, with good quality models from $200 to $3,000. As I mentioned earlier, you may be surprised at how inexpensive it is to rent an upright acoustic piano monthly while learning. You can also find great deals on keyboards and pianos on *eBay, Craigslist,* and other sites.

Additional Costs: Consider costs for accessories such as stands, benches, pedals, and headphones—factor in potential costs for lessons, maintenance, and tuning for acoustic pianos.

Long-Term Investment: Think about the long-term value. A more expensive, higher-quality instrument might be a better investment if you are committed to learning and improving.

SPACE: Evaluate the space where you will place the instrument. Acoustic pianos, especially grand pianos, require substantial room. Upright pianos and digital pianos need less space.

Environment: Ensure the environment is suitable, avoiding places with extreme temperatures or humidity.
Digital pianos are more resilient in varying conditions compared to acoustic pianos.

Storage and Mobility: If space is limited, consider a digital piano or keyboard you can quickly move or store when not in use.

PORTABILITY: A lightweight digital piano or keyboard is ideal if you plan to move the instrument frequently. Acoustic pianos are heavy and difficult to move.

Transportation Needs: Consider how you will transport the instrument for lessons, gigs, or practice sessions outside your home. Keyboards are typically more portable and convenient for these purposes.

MAINTENANCE

Acoustic Pianos: Require regular tuning (typically twice a year) and occasional repairs. Proper care includes dusting, covering, and avoiding exposure to extreme conditions.

Digital Pianos and Keyboards are generally low maintenance. Keep them clean and protect them from spills and dust. Be prepared to update software for digital pianos with advanced features.

Longevity: Consider the instrument's longevity. Acoustic pianos, when properly maintained, can last decades. Digital pianos have a shorter lifespan but require less frequent maintenance.

SOUND QUALITY

Acoustic Pianos are known for their rich, resonant sound, which can vary based on the piano's make, model, and condition.

Digital Pianos: Sound quality has improved significantly, with many models offering high-fidelity samples of acoustic pianos. Look for models with weighted keys and advanced sound engines.

Keyboards and Synthesizers: Offer a wide range of sounds and effects. Ensure the keyboard has good sound quality and feel, which can vary significantly between models.

TIPS FOR BUYING USED INSTRUMENTS

Recently, I helped a nightclub purchase a grand piano for their piano bar. They wanted a great piano but did not want to spend too much money. I found a used *Yamaha C3* Conservatory Grand Piano. It was beat up. We needed to fix the action and replace some pads, hammers, and strings. The sale price worked for us because it was low enough to pay for maintenance and still get a good deal.

Look for scratches, dents, or chips on the body and keys. Check the pedals and the condition of the piano's finish. For acoustic pianos, examine the strings, hammers, and soundboard for cracks or signs of damage. For digital pianos and keyboards, ensure all buttons, knobs, and connections are intact and functioning. If you're spending a lot of money on a piano, bring in a piano tuner who can see if it has a cracked soundboard. Ensure that the piano or keyboard stands securely and has no loose parts affecting performance. Check for consistency in sound and touch across all keys. Listen for any buzzing, rattling, or muted sounds indicating issues. Test the sustain, soft, and sostenuto pedals on an acoustic piano to ensure that they work smoothly and effectively. Test various sounds and effects on digital pianos and keyboards. Ensure the audio output is free of distortions or malfunctions.

NEGOTIATING PRICE

Know the average price range for your desired specific model. Websites like *eBay, Craigslist,* and musical instrument retailers can provide insights. Adjust your offer based on the instrument's condition, age, and any apparent needed repairs. If you purchase a legacy name-brand piano, it may be worth it to put a little extra money into restoring the instrument. Be prepared to negotiate. Use any flaws or potential repairs as leverage to lower the price. Set a maximum price you are willing to pay and stick to it.

———

CHECKING MAINTENANCE HISTORY

I've found that most people do not keep maintenance records on their instruments, so don't be discouraged if they have none. Ask for any maintenance records or documentation of repairs. Regular tuning records for acoustic pianos are a good sign of proper care. Find out how many owners the instrument has had and the reasons for selling. Consider hiring a piano technician or a knowledgeable musician to inspect the instrument before purchasing.

UNDERSTANDING RETURN POLICIES

Confirm the seller's return policy, especially if you buy from a retailer. Understand the time frame and conditions under which you can return the instrument. Check if any remaining warranty is transferable. For digital instruments, manufacturer warranties on specific parts might still be valid. Negotiate a trial period if you can... to test the instrument in your home environment before committing to the purchase.

SECTION TWO
SETTING UP YOUR PRACTICE SPACE

"If I don't practice for a day, I know it. If I don't practice for two days, the critics know it. And if I don't practice for three days, the public knows it." – Louis Armstrong

Louis Armstrong
Credit – Wikimedia Commons

While I've found that I can practice anywhere if I am not disturbing anyone around me, I've also learned that you can significantly enhance your learning experience with the right conditions. The beauty of it all is that you have the power to create these conditions, adapting your practice environment to suit your preferences.

ERGONOMIC SEATING

Choose an adjustable piano bench, allowing you to sit with your feet flat on the floor and your knees slightly below the level of the keyboard. Ensure that your back is straight, and your elbows are at a comfortable height. A well-padded bench will provide comfort during extended practice sessions. Use a footrest to achieve the proper seating height and angle if necessary.

If you're in a studio situation sitting at a desk or using a stand with a keyboard in front of you, find a very comfortable office chair with no arms that raises and lowers. In the studio, I find that I'm moving around when I'm doing my production. When you become proficient at recording, learning macro prompts on PRO TOOLS or your preferred software lets you record your performance easily. Still, when practicing, you need a comfortable chair that adjusts to the desk or stand you use to play your keyboard.

PROPER LIGHTING

Proper lighting is not just about avoiding eye strain, it's about enhancing your practice experience. Position your piano or keyboard near a source of natural light, such as a window, to take advantage of daylight. If natural light is insufficient, use an adjustable lamp to illuminate your sheet music and keyboard. Avoid placing lights directly behind you, as this can cause glare on the sheet music. Instead, aim for even, diffused lighting that reduces shadows and highlights the keys and music stand clearly. This will not only protect your eyes but also keep you engaged and focused on your practice.

The better you become, the less you will depend upon lighting. Your hands will know where to go on the piano. If **Stevie Wonder** can do it in such a fantastic way, we can do it with practice, too!

"Blind don't mean you can't, you know, listen. Ya gots to work with what you gots to work with." – Stevie Wonder

Stevie Wonder
Credit – Wikimedia Commons

MINIMIZING DISTRACTIONS

Choose a quiet room where you can close the door to block out noise from other areas of your home. Inform family members or housemates of your practice schedule to minimize interruptions. Remove or silence electronic devices that can cause distractions, such as phones, tablets, and televisions. Keeping your practice area tidy and organized can also create a conducive environment for concentration.

If you practice with a keyboard with a headphone jack, use headphones to practice anytime in silence without affecting anyone around you.

GOOD VENTILATION

Proper airflow prevents the buildup of moisture and dust while helping maintain a consistent temperature, which can affect your comfort and the condition of your instrument. Choose a room with windows you can open for fresh air if possible. Alternatively, fans or air purifiers can improve air circulation. Avoid placing your piano or keyboard in areas with direct exposure to heating or cooling vents, as extreme temperature changes can damage the instrument. Breathing exercises help you maintain calm and mindfulness throughout practice sessions.

ACOUSTIC CONSIDERATIONS

Carpeting, curtains, and upholstered furniture can help absorb sound and reduce echo, creating a more pleasant acoustic environment. For digital pianos and keyboards, ensure you have quality headphones or speakers to monitor your playing accurately. Consider using soundproofing materials if noise levels are a concern, especially if you live in an apartment or shared housing. Positioning your piano or keyboard away from walls and corners can also help improve sound quality.

ESSENTIAL ACCESSORIES

In addition to your instrument, ideally, you should have a handful of accessories at your disposal in your practice space:

A MUSIC STAND helps maintain good posture and keeps your hands free to play. Built-in stands are common for acoustic pianos, but a separate adjustable stand can be useful for digital pianos and keyboards. Some keyboards provide attachable sheet music stands. Look for sturdy stands with adjustable height and angle to suit different playing positions and lighting conditions.

A METRONOME helps musicians practice at a consistent tempo and can be set to various speeds to accommodate different pieces. Traditional mechanical metronomes are reliable and easy to use. In contrast, digital metronomes often offer additional features like different time signatures and sound options. Many digital pianos and keyboard apps also include built-in metronomes.

If you have a somewhat sophisticated setup, you can use a click track from your recording software in place of a metronome. Although this is becoming a relic of the past, some free-standing drum machines also work well to keep time.

PEDALS add expressiveness and dynamic control to piano playing. The sustain (damper), soft (una corda), and sostenuto pedals are standard for acoustic pianos. Digital pianos and keyboards may come with a single sustain pedal, but upgrading to a three-pedal unit can enhance the playing experience. Ensure the pedals are compatible with your instrument and offer a realistic response.

If you're working with an acoustic piano, you already have pedals. Some acoustic pianos only provide two pedals: a sustain pedal (on the right) and a soft pedal (on the left). Acoustic pianos with three pedals provide the sostenuto pedal in the center. I've rarely used this pedal in my career, as it sustains the bottom end while leaving the higher keys staccato for chording with the left hand while soloing with the right.

HEADPHONES
Look for headphones that provide clear, accurate sound and are comfortable for extended use. Over-ear models with noise isolation are ideal, as they help minimize external distractions and allow you to focus on your playing.

RECORDING EQUIPMENT:
Basic setups include a digital recorder or a smartphone with a good microphone. More advanced setups involve audio interfaces, studio microphones, and computer software for editing and mixing. Regularly recording yourself helps identify areas for improvement and track progress over time.

Many easy-to-use standalone digital recorders are available for recording at low prices for beginners.

ORGANIZING A PRACTICE ROUTINE
The most essential element in learning to play an instrument is repetition. Practicing your craft is the only way you will get better. Create a performance mindset. Establish a routine that works for you. Don't be afraid of feedback or critique. Feed on it! The great pianist **Art Tatum** became arguably the most accomplished jazz pianist of his time. After fifty years, he wanted another fifty years to get better. He knew you could continuously improve, no matter how good you are.

"Perfection is not attainable, but if we chase perfection, we can catch excellence." – Art Tatum

Art Tatum

SCHEDULE PRACTICE TIME

Aim to practice daily, even for a shorter duration, to maintain and build your skills. Start with manageable sessions, such as 30 minutes to an hour, and gradually increase as you improve your stamina and focus. Allocate specific times during the day when you are least likely to be interrupted and try to stick to these times to build a routine.

SET REALISTIC GOALS: Break down larger objectives into smaller, manageable tasks. For instance, aim to master a specific piece of music, improve a particular technique, or understand a new concept in music theory. **Goals should be specific, measurable, attainable, relevant, and time-bound (SMART)**. Review your goals on a regular basis and adjust if necessary to reflect your progress and new challenges.

KEEP A PRACTICE JOURNAL: Record details of each practice session, including the pieces or exercises worked on, specific goals, challenges encountered, and any breakthroughs. Reflecting on past entries can help identify patterns in your practice habits and celebrate your progress. Additionally, jotting down practice tips and feedback from teachers can be beneficial.

DO WARM-UP EXERCISES: Start with gentle finger and hand stretches to increase flexibility. Follow this with technical exercises such as scales, arpeggios, and finger independence drills. These activities help to develop finger strength, agility, and coordination, setting a solid foundation for the main practice session.

DO COOL-DOWN ROUTINES: Spend the last few minutes of your practice playing something familiar and enjoyable at a slower pace. Gentle hand and finger stretches can also help to release any tension built up during practice. This exercise not only aids in recovery but also leaves you feeling positive and ready for the next session.

Performing and practicing is as much in the mind as it is a physical activity. The great cellist **Yo-Yo Ma** said:

"Practicing is not only playing your instrument, either by yourself or rehearsing with others – it also includes imagining yourself practicing. Your brain forms the same neural connections and muscle memory whether you are imagining the task or actually doing it."

Yo-Yo Ma
Credit – Wikimedia Commons

SECTION THREE
BASIC MUSIC THEORY

Some of the most excellent musicians could not read a note. Legendary jazz pianist **Errol Garner** was among these. **Paul McCartney** wrote a string of hits before he learned the essence of music theory. You are light-years ahead of anyone else if you have a great ear. Still, it is essential to learn music theory if you want to accelerate your learning experience. Grasping basic concepts of music theory helps you understand music on a different level. Like a child learning to speak a new language, you will absorb concepts and techniques that provide a foundation for greatness. It's not just about sight-reading and soloing, but also about accompaniment and a myriad of other reasons.

There was a time when I saw music theory as the 'work' part of learning an instrument, with everything else being the 'fun' part. But as the great composer **Claude Debussy** once said:

"Works of art make rules; rules do not make works of art."

So, you might ask, why should I bother with the 'tedium' of music theory? After all, I'm an artist! My simple answer is this: the more you know, the more effortlessly you can create. And you'll soon discover that this knowledge is not just worth it, but invaluable!

Claude Debussy
Credit – Wikimedia Commons

INTRODUCTION TO NOTES AND SCALES

Music is math. Theory and harmony provide the foundation for a greater understanding of music, just as Geometry does to architecture and Calculus to computer programming. The knowledge you gain provides a benchmark for critical thinking. You use it in more ways than you would ever imagine without knowing it!

NOTES ON A PIANO: Before you ever learn how to read sheet music, familiarize yourself with notes as they appear on the piano keyboard. The piano keyboard has twelve keys in a repeating pattern: seven white keys and five black keys. White keys on a piano represent the alphabet's first letters (A, B, C, D, E, F, G). Black keys are named using sharps (#) and flats (b).

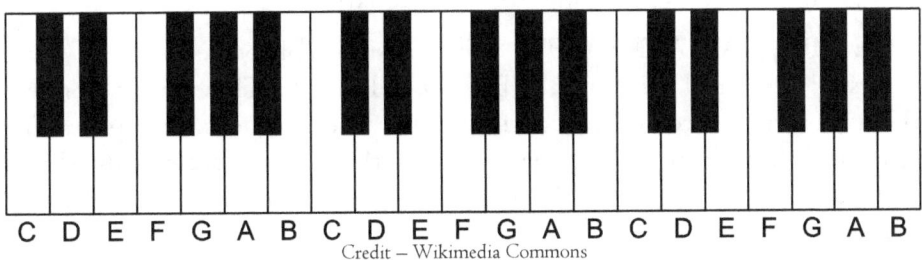

Credit – Wikimedia Commons

IDENTIFY MIDDLE C

Locate the Groups of Black Keys: Black keys are laid out in groups of twos and threes, and this pattern repeats across the keyboard.

Find Middle C: Middle C is the white key directly to the left of the group of two black keys closest to the keyboard's middle. It is often marked on beginner keyboards and is a central reference point for finding other notes.

FIND THE WHITE KEYS

C Note: All C notes are located to the immediate left of the groups of two black keys. Middle C is the most central C note.

D Note: D is found between the two black keys.

E Note: E is the white key to the right of the two black keys.

F Note: F is located to the immediate left of the groups of three black keys.

G Note: G is the second white key in the group of three black keys.

A Note: A is the third white key in the group of three black keys.

B Note: B is the white key to the right of the three black keys.

FIND THE BLACK KEYS

Sharp (#) and Flat (b) Notes: Black keys are named based on their adjacent white keys. When viewing a black key to the right of a white key, it is considered a sharp, while a black key to the left is considered a flat. Look at the key signature first to see whether the song is written in sharps or flats.

Example: The black key between C and D can be called C# (C sharp) or Db(D flat).

PRACTICE TIPS

Use Visual Aids: Stickers or markers can help beginners identify notes.

Memorize Patterns: Regularly practicing finding and naming notes helps reinforce memory.

Play Simple Songs: To familiarize yourself with the keyboard layout, start with simple songs that use a limited range of notes.

By understanding the keyboard's structure and using these steps, beginners can quickly learn to find and identify notes on the piano. Regular practice and visual aids can further aid in mastering the keyboard layout.

THE MUSICAL ALPHABET: The musical alphabet consists of seven letters, as mentioned previously: A, B, C, D, E, F, and G. These letters represent the seven natural notes within an octave. After G, the sequence repeats, starting again at A. In addition to these natural notes, there are five accidentals (sharps and flats) that fill in the gaps, making a total of 12 unique notes in Western music:

A, A#/Bb, B, C, C#/Db, D, D#/Eb, E, F, F#/Gb, G, and G#/Ab.

MAJOR SCALES: A major scale is a sequence of seven notes forming a specific pattern of whole and half steps. The pattern is: whole, whole, half, whole, whole, whole, half. The C major scale is the simplest example, as it uses only the white keys on the piano:

- C, D, E, F, G, A, B, C

The major scale has a bright and happy sound and is the foundation for many Western music compositions.

MINOR SCALES, with their darker and more melancholic sound, contrast major scales. Three types of minor scales exist: natural, harmonic, and melodic.

Natural Minor Scale: Follows the pattern: whole, half, whole, whole, half, whole, whole. Example in A minor:

- A, B, C, D, E, F, G, A

Harmonic Minor Scale: Similar to a natural minor scale but with a raised seventh note. Example in A (harmonic minor):

- A, B, C, D, E, F, G♯, A

Melodic Minor Scale: Ascends with a raised sixth and seventh note but descends like the natural minor. Example in A (melodic minor ascending):

- A, B, C, D, E, F♯, G♯, A
- Descending: A, G, F, E, D, C, B, A

CHROMATIC SCALES: A chromatic scale includes all twelve notes within an octave, each a half step apart. This scale uses every key on the piano, both white and black. The chromatic scale helps develop finger strength and dexterity. Example:

- C, C♯, D, D♯, E, F, F♯, G, G♯, A, A♯, B, C

A PENTATONIC SCALE is a five-note scale used in many musical genres, including folk, rock, and blues. There are major and minor pentatonic scales.

Major Pentatonic Scale: First, second, third, fifth, and sixth notes of the major scale. Example in C major pentatonic:

- C, D, E, G, A, C

Minor Pentatonic Scale: First, third, fourth, fifth, and seventh notes of the natural minor scale. Example in A minor pentatonic:

- A, C, D, E, G, A

Pentatonic scales are easy to learn and play, making them great for improvisation.

Mastering these fundamentals will significantly enhance your musical journey. At first, this may all seem overwhelming, as will any new learning experience. Take the time to learn notes and scales and work on them individually during your practice sessions. Learning the different scales and where the notes exist on the keyboard will quickly give you the basics of translating music theory to the piano keyboard before we go further. Work on this first step and be comfortable with it before you move on.

"Be your own artist, and always be confident in what you're doing. If you're not going to be confident, you might as well not be doing it."
— Aretha Franklin

Aretha Franklin
Credit – Wikimedia Commons

UNDERSTANDING RHYTHM AND TIMING- NOTE VALUES

Note values indicate the duration of each note, showing how long you should hold a key down. Here are the basic note values:

- **Whole Note** : Held for four beats.

- **Half Note.** : Held for two beats.

- **Quarter Note** : Held for one beat.

- **Eighth Note** : Held for half a beat.

- **Sixteenth Note** : Held for a quarter of a beat.

Each note value has a corresponding rest, which indicates a period of silence for the same duration.

TIME SIGNATURES

Time signatures consist of the number of beats in each measure and the note value that gets the beat. The most common time signatures are:

- **4/4 Time**: Common time means four beats per measure; the quarter note gets one beat.
- **3/4 Time**: Three beats per measure. Quarter note gets one beat, often used in waltzes.
- **2/4 Time**: Two beats per measure. Quarter note gets one beat, commonly used in marches.
- **6/8 Time**: Six beats per measure, with the eighth note getting one beat, creating a lilting feel often used in folk and classical music.

SYNCOPATION involves emphasizing beats or parts of beats that are usually unaccented, creating a sense of surprise and rhythmic variation. It's commonly used in jazz, pop, and dance music. Syncopation can be achieved by accenting off-beats, using rests on strong beats, or tying notes across beats.

TEMPO is the speed of the music, measured in beats per minute (BPM). Common tempo markings include:

- **Largo**: Very slow (40-60 BPM)
- **Adagio**: Slow and stately (66-76 BPM)
- **Andante**: Walking pace (76-108 BPM)
- **Moderato**: Moderate speed (108-120 BPM)
- **Allegro**: Fast, quick, and bright (120-168 BPM)
- **Presto**: Very fast (168-200 BPM)

Practicing with a metronome improves your internal sense of timing and rhythm. Start with a comfortable tempo, gradually increasing the speed. Ensure each note is played evenly in time with the metronome. Practice with different time signatures and rhythms to build versatility.

READING SHEET MUSIC

Although you should absolutely learn to read sheet music, many professional musicians use chord charts that consist of lettered chords (such as CM for C Major or Gm for G Minor) placed within measures on a lead sheet, sometimes with a melody line. Orchestral and band charts are usually crafted as standard sheet music, and good reading skills are essential for professional musicians.

"You can't knock on opportunity's door and not be ready."
— Bruno Mars

Bruno Mars
Credit – Wikimedia Commons

TREBLE AND BASS CLEFS

TREBLE CLEF

The treble clef is also referred to as the G clef. It represents higher-pitched notes typically played with the right hand. The symbol loops around the second line of the staff, indicating that this line is the note G.

The notes on the lines are E, G, B, D, and F, from bottom to top, remembered by the phrase "Every Good Boy Does Fine." The spaces spell out the word "FACE."

BASS CLEF

The bass clef is also called to as the F clef. the bass clef is used for lower-pitched notes typically played with the left hand. The symbol has two dots surrounding the fourth line of the staff, indicating that this line is the note F. Notes on the lines are G, B, D, F, and A, from bottom to top, remembered by the phrase "Good Boys Do Fine Always." The spaces spell out "All Cows Eat Grass."

KEY SIGNATURES – EXAMPLE -
B FLAT AND E FLAT (KEY OF Bb major or G minor)

Key signatures establish the musical key of a piece by indicating which notes are to be played as sharps or flats throughout the piece. The key signature exists right after the clef at the beginning of the staff.

- **Sharps (♯)**: Each sharp raises a note by a half step. For example, an F♯ is played instead of an F.
- **Flats (♭)**: Each flat lowers a note by a half step. For example, a B♭ is played instead of a B.

The key signature helps you quickly identify the piece's key and which notes are altered.

DYNAMICS in music indicate the volume at which the music should be played. Standard dynamic markings include:

- **p (piano)**: Soft
- **mp (mezzo-piano)**: Moderately soft
- **mf (mezzo-forte)**: Moderately loud
- **f (forte)**: Loud
- **pp (pianissimo)**: Very soft
- **ff (fortissimo)**: Very loud
- **cresc. (crescendo)**: Gradually getting louder
- **dim. (diminuendo)**: Gradually getting softer

ARTICULATIONS provide instructions on how individual notes or phrases should be played. Common articulations include:

- **Staccato (.)**: Play the note short and detached.
- **Legato (−)**: Play the notes smoothly and connect them.
- **Accent (>)**: Emphasize the note.
- **Tenuto (−)**: Hold the note for its total value.

COMMON SYMBOLS

In addition to dynamics and articulations, there are several other common symbols in sheet music:

- **Repeat Signs (:|)**: Indicates that a section should be repeated.
- **Fermata (⌢)**: Hold the note longer than its usual value.
- **Slurs**: Indicate that notes should be played smoothly together.
- **Ties**: Connects two notes of the same pitch, combining their durations.

If you understand clefs, key signatures, dynamics, articulations, and common musical symbols, you are halfway there. These elements provide the necessary instructions for interpreting and performing a piece of music accurately. But remember, it's not just about understanding these components. Regular practice and familiarization with them are key to enhancing your ability to read and play music effectively. So, keep practicing, and you'll see the improvement.

This is the part of learning that you need to complete to enjoy playing effortlessly. In the next chapter, we will start to put this all together and show you basic playing techniques. If you take the time to learn the basics of music theory first, the next steps will come much easier. Stay with it!

My friend **Rod Stewart** is a *Billboard Multi-Platinum* artist and songwriter with many hits over decades. It didn't come easy for him, but he persisted and prevailed.

"Songwriting's never been a natural art for me; it's always been a bit of a struggle." — Rod Stewart

Tad Sisler with Rod Stewart
Source- Sisler Private Collection

CHAPTER TWO
BASIC TECHNIQUES
ARTIST SPOTLIGHT
DONALD FAGEN

Donald **Fagen** composed what could be argued as the most sophisticated pop music of his time. Along with his writing and performing partner Walter **Becker**, they formed **Steely Dan**. They changed perceptions of the limits of popular music. His learning experience was different than most. He said:

"I took some lessons as a kid but trained myself by ear. I did it the way jazz musicians used to learn years ago, which is to play records and slow them down to figure out the notes. At first, I tried to imitate Red Garland, who was my favorite jazz pianist."

Donald Fagen started with the rudiments of basic playing techniques and then expanded upon them by training his ear. Like a road map, many ways exist to reach a single destination. This chapter is intended to give the reader the most equipped vehicle to reach your first destination: to play a song effortlessly.

Donald Fagen
Credit – Wikimedia Commons

SECTION ONE
FINGER PLACEMENT AND HAND POSITIONING
CORRECT FINGER PLACEMENT: My mother emphasized that I should always play with my fingertips, and in doing so, I would gain greater dexterity.

HOME POSITION: The home position is the starting point for correct finger placement on the piano. It helps beginners develop good habits and ensures they can play efficiently and comfortably.

MIDDLE C POSITION: Place your right-hand thumb on Middle C (the C note nearest the center of the keyboard). Naturally let your other fingers fall on subsequent white keys:

- Thumb (1) on C
- Index finger (2) on D
- Middle finger (3) on E
- Ring finger (4) on F
- Pinky finger (5) on G

Similarly, for the left hand:

- Pinky (5) on the C below Middle C
- Ring finger (4) on D
- Middle finger (3) on E
- Index finger (2) on F
- Thumb (1) on G

PROPER HAND SHAPE: Your fingers should be curved as if holding a small ball, and your wrists should be level with the keyboard. This position helps in avoiding tension and promotes fluid movement across the keys.

FINGER NUMBERING is vital for reading music and following fingerings in sheet music. The numbering system is as follows:

- Thumb = 1
- Index Finger = 2
- Middle Finger = 3
- Ring Finger = 4
- Pinky Finger = 5

Both hands use this same numbering system, which helps coordinate and transition smoothly between notes.

FINGER STRENGTH EXERCISES

Five-Finger Scales: Play up and down the scale using only the five fingers in the home position. Start slowly and increase speed as you get comfortable.

Hanon Exercises are classical piano exercises designed to build finger strength and independence. Start with simple exercises. Gradually progress to more complex patterns.

Finger Push-Ups: Place your fingers on a table or hard surface and press down, lifting the palm of your hand slightly. This exercise strengthens your fingers and hand muscles.

COORDINATION DRILLS

Hands Together Scales: Practice playing scales with both hands simultaneously. Start with simple scales and gradually include more complex ones.

Contrary Motion Scales: Play scales with both hands moving in opposite directions. This exercise helps in developing independent hand movement.

Chord Progressions: Practice playing simple chord progressions with both hands. Start with basic triads and move to more complex chord shapes.

Robert Moog invented the first great analog wave synthesizer. He looked at life in a different way than most. He described the human brain playing piano as follows:

> *"When a pianist sits down and does a virtuoso performance, he is, in a technical sense, transmitting more information to a machine than any other human activity involving machinery allows."*

Our brains are amazing!

PROPER HAND POSITIONING

As a young man, I marvelled at the accomplished pianists I could witness. In my twenties, I met **Joe Massters**, a great jazz pianist. **Joe** had been performing for many years and was in his seventies. Joe's hands were failing him, and it was painful for him to play the intricate jazz solos and changes he was known for. He cried to me one night, saying he wished he had paid more attention to nurturing his hands through the years. Perhaps it was more arthritis than improper hand positioning that led him to where he was. Still, his statement made me take hand positioning more seriously as a young performer.

RELAXED HANDS:

Tension in the hands can lead to discomfort and fatigue, making playing difficult for extended periods. Keep your hands loose and relaxed by shaking them out regularly and avoiding gripping the keys too tightly. To avoid stress, ensure your shoulders are relaxed, elbows are slightly bent, and wrists are level with the keyboard. Take frequent breaks during practice to shake out any stiffness and focus on maintaining a relaxed posture.

Joanna Hodges' method made us so confident in our knowledge of any given piece that we could relax into our performances in competitions and nail it!

HAND POSTURE EXERCISES

Specific exercises can help maintain proper hand posture and build strength and flexibility. Here are a few practical exercises:

Spider Exercise: Place your hands on the keyboard, play one note with each finger, and lift each finger independently while keeping the others down. This exercise helps in developing finger independence and control.

Five-Finger Scales: As you did for finger strength, play scales using only the five fingers in the home position, focusing on keeping the fingers curved and the hand relaxed.

Hand Stretching: Stretch your fingers gently before and after playing to keep them flexible and prevent stiffness.

> *"If you want to play better and live longer, you have to find a good posture." — Sir András Schiff*

PREVENTING STRAIN

Ensure your bench height allows for a natural hand position with your forearms parallel to the ground. Warm up before practicing with gentle stretches and finger exercises and avoid playing through pain or discomfort. If you feel any strain, stop playing and rest your hands. Relax into your performances; if you like what you are doing, you will better enjoy the experience!

My old friend, iconic entertainer **Trini Lopez** had a string of hits, and he was a favorite of **President John F. Kennedy**. Trini said:

"Everything is attitude. It's very important to always like what you're doing."

Tad Sisler with Trini Lopez
Source – Sisler Private Collection

COMMON MISTAKES TO AVOID

FLAT FINGERS: Playing with flat fingers means pressing the keys with the flat part of the finger rather than the fingertip. This exercise can reduce control and dexterity, making it harder to play smoothly and accurately. Ensure your fingers are naturally curved as if holding a small ball and use your fingertips to press the keys. Regular practice of five-finger exercises can help reinforce this habit.

TENSE WRISTS: Tension in the wrists can lead to discomfort, fatigue, and even injury. It restricts fluid movement and can negatively impact the overall quality of playing. Keep your wrists relaxed and level with the keyboard. During practice breaks, shake out your hands and wrists regularly to check for tension. Ensure that your bench height allows your forearms to be parallel to the floor.

OVERSTRETCHING: Overstretching occurs when trying to reach keys that are too far apart, causing strain on the hands and fingers. Overstretching can lead to discomfort and potential injury. Use proper finger positioning and hand movement to reach keys instead of stretching your fingers too far. Practice your scales and arpeggios to gradually improve reach without straining.

INCORRECT THUMB POSITIONING: Placing the thumb incorrectly, such as using the flat part or bending it awkwardly, can hinder movement and cause strain.

Use the side tip of the thumb to press keys, keeping it relaxed and slightly bent. Practice thumb-under techniques for scales and arpeggios to ensure smooth transitions between notes.

POOR POSTURE: Poor posture, slouching, or sitting too far from the keyboard can lead to back pain and make playing more challenging.
 Sit on the edge of a properly adjusted bench with feet flat on the floor. Keep your back straight, shoulders relaxed, and elbows at a comfortable height relative to the keyboard.

"When you play, never mind who listens to you." — Robert Schumann

Robert Schumann
Credit — Wikimedia Commons

SECTION TWO
BASIC CHORDS AND PROGRESSIONS

When I first became a professional performer, every night when I sat down at the piano, I would 'discover' a variation on a chord, adding notes here and there to beautify the sound. **Paul McCartney** famously said that he learned a handful of chords when he was young and wrote a few songs. Then, one day, another musician showed him how to play a minor chord, which changed his life! Adding a seventh, ninth, or eleventh enhances a chord. Playing a major seventh is gorgeous. Performing a minor seventh can make you sad or reflective. You have the power to move people when you know chords.

MAJOR CHORDS: A major chord has three notes: the root, the major third, and the perfect fifth. It is built by stacking two intervals — a major third (four half steps) and a minor third (three half steps). Major chords have a bright and happy sound.
•Example: C major chord (C-E-G).

MINOR CHORDS: A minor chord also has three notes: the root, minor third, and perfect fifth. It is built by stacking a minor third (three half steps) and a major third (four half steps). Minor chords produce a sad and melancholy sound.
•Example: A minor chord (A-C-E).

TRIADS: A triad is a chord with three notes: a root, third, and fifth.
Major Triad: Root + Major third + Perfect fifth.
•Example: G major triad (G-B-D).

Minor Triad: Root + Minor third + Perfect fifth.
•Example: D minor triad (D-F-A).

INVERSIONS rearrange the notes of a chord so that different notes have the lowest pitch.
First Inversion: The lowest note is the "middle" or third of the chord.
•Example: C major in first inversion (E-G-C).
Second Inversion: The lowest note is the "end" or fifth of the chord.
•Example: C major in second inversion (G-C-E).

CHORD VOICINGS: Chord voicing refers to the arrangement of the notes in a chord and the octave in which they are played. Different voicings can create a varied and rich sound.
Closed Voicing: All notes of the chord are within an octave.
•Example: C major closed voicing (C-E-G).
Open Voicing: Notes are spread out over more than an octave.
•Example: C major open voicing (C-G-E).

PRACTICE EXERCISES
Chord Drills: Practice playing major and minor chords using different keys up and down the keyboard.
Inversion Exercises: Play each chord in the root position, first and second inversion.
Voicing Variations: Experiment with closed and open voicings for the same chord.

COMMON CHORD PATTERNS
I-IV-V-I: This pattern is fundamental in Western music and is found in many classical, pop, and rock songs.
•Example in C major: C (I) - F (IV) - G (V) - C (I).
ii-V-I: Common in jazz, this progression creates a smooth and satisfying resolution.
•Example in C major: Dm (ii) - G (V) - C (I).
vi-IV-I-V: Popular in modern pop music, often called the "Axis of Awesome" progression.
•Example in C major: Am (vi) - F (IV) - C (I) - G (V).

"There, in the chords and melodies, is everything I want to say. The words just jolly it along. It's always been my way of expressing what, for me, is inexpressible by any other means." — David Bowie

---

David Bowie
Credit – Wikimedia Commons

COMMON CHORD PROGRESSIONS
In popular music the most common progression is the I-IV-V progression.

I-IV-V PROGRESSION: The I-IV-V progression is one of Western music's most fundamental and frequently used chord progressions. It consists of the first (I), fourth (IV), and fifth (V) chords of a key.

Example in C major: C (I) - F (IV) - G (V)

This progression has a strong, pleasing, and harmonious sound, making it ideal for many songs across genres such as rock, pop, and classical. Many piano courses for beginners boast they can get you to play 100 songs or more within a week on the piano. Playing many songs very quickly can easily be done using the most common chord progression, I-IV-V, or one, four five. For instance:

THREE POPULAR SONGS CONTAINING THE I-IV-V PROGRESSION
"Twist and Shout" by The Beatles
Chord Progression in Key of D: D (I) - G (IV) - A (V)
This classic rock song uses the I-IV-V progression throughout, making it a great example of how powerful and catchy this simple progression can be.

"La Bamba" by Ritchie Valens
Chord Progression in Key of C: C (I) - F (IV) - G (V)
It is a famous rock and roll song that relies heavily on the I-IV-V chord progression, creating an energetic and danceable rhythm.

"Hound Dog" by Elvis Presley
Chord Progression in Key of C: C (I) - F (IV) - G (V)
This iconic rock and roll hit is another example of the I-IV-V progression, providing a solid and straightforward harmonic foundation.

These songs are great examples of how the I-IV-V chord progression can be used across various genres to create memorable and enduring music.

●●●●●●●●●

ii-V-I PROGRESSION: The ii-V-I progression is found primarily in jazz music. It provides a smooth and satisfying resolution. It consists of the second (ii), fifth (V), and first (I) chords of a key.

Example in C major: Dm (ii) - G (V) - C (I)

This progression is jazzy and sophisticated, often used in jazz standards and improvisations.

THREE POPULAR SONGS CONTAINING THE ii-V-I PROGRESSION

"Autumn Leaves"

Progression Example: Cm7 (ii) - F7 (V) - BbMaj7 (I)

The jazz standard beautifully incorporates the ii-V-I progression, especially in its chord changes.

"Misty" by Erroll Garner

Progression Example: Gm7 (ii) - C7 (V) - FMaj7 (I)

It is a well-loved jazz ballad that frequently uses the ii-V-I progression, creating smooth and flowing harmonic movement.

"All the Things You Are" by Oscar Hammerstein II and Jerome Kern

Progression Example: F#m7 (ii) - B7 (V) - EMaj7 (I)

This song is a jazz standard that features the ii-V-I progression in several key changes throughout the piece.

These songs are excellent examples of how the ii-V-I progression can create smooth, cohesive, and pleasing harmonic progressions in jazz and popular music.

ARTIST SPOTLIGHT
DIANA KRALL

Diana Krall is a Canadian jazz pianist and singer and one of the most successful jazz artists of her generation. Her smooth vocals and sophisticated piano playing, combining jazz with contemporary interpretation, has wowed audiences for decades. I've always felt when I play a song that everyone in the audience hearing it has their own unique memory of this song; what they were doing when they first heard it, or does it remind them of an early romance, or a beautiful day walking on the beach, or laughing with friends? **Diana** coined my feeling perfectly when she said:

"You're creating an intimacy that everybody feels, that it's their experience, not yours. I'll never introduce a song and say, now this song is about 'my' broken heart."

Always remember that the song is the focus, and the emotion and passion you put into your rendition makes you the perfect messenger.

Diana Krall

vi-IV-I-V PROGRESSION: Also known as the "Axis of Awesome" progression, the vi-IV-I-V is prevalent in modern pop music. It consists of the sixth (vi), fourth (IV), first (I), and fifth (V) chords of a key.

Example in C major: Am (vi) - F (IV) - C (I) - G (V)

This progression is catchy and memorable, commonly found in many hit songs.

THREE POPULAR SONGS CONTAINING THE vi-IV-I-V PROGRESSION

"Let It Be" by The Beatles

Chord Progression: Am (vi) - F (IV) - C (I) - G (V)

One of The Beatles' most famous songs, "Let It Be," uses this progression, creating a soothing and memorable melody.

"With or Without You" by U2

Chord Progression: D (vi) - A (IV) - Bm (I) - G (V)

U2's iconic ballad "With or Without You" prominently uses this progression, enhancing its emotional and uplifting atmosphere.

"Africa" by Toto

Chord Progression: Bm (vi) - G (IV) - D (I) - A (V)

This enduring hit by Toto employs the vi-IV-I-V progression, giving it a driving yet harmonious sound.

••••••••••

BLUES PROGRESSION: The 12-bar blues progression is fundamental in blues music and has influenced many other genres, including rock and jazz. It typically uses the I, IV, and V chords in a specific sequence over 12 measures.

Example in C major:

- Measure 1-4: C (I)

- Measure 5-6: F (IV)
- Measure 7-8: C (I)
- Measure 9: G (V)
- Measure 10: F (IV)
- Measure 11-12: C (I)

This progression has a soulful and rhythmic feel, forming the basis of countless blues songs.

THREE POPULAR SONGS USING THE 12-BAR BLUES PROGRESSION

"Johnny B. Goode" by Chuck Berry

Chord Progression in A: A (I) - A (I) - A (I) - A (I) - D (IV) - D (IV) - A (I) - A (I) - E (V) - D (IV) - A (I) - E (V)

This iconic rock and roll song is built around the 12-bar blues progression, featuring Chuck Berry's signature guitar riffs and energetic performance.

"Sweet Home Chicago" by Robert Johnson

Chord Progression in E: E (I) - E (I) - E (I) - E (I) - A (IV) - A (IV) - E (I) - E (I) - B (V) - A (IV) - E (I) - B (V)

A classic blues song by Robert Johnson, covered by numerous artists. This song remains a blues standard. The 12-bar blues progression forms the backbone of the music.

"Pride and Joy" by Stevie Ray Vaughan

Chord Progression in E: E (I) - E (I) - E (I) - E (I) - A (IV) - A (IV) - E (I) - E (I) - B (V) - A (IV) - E (I) - E (I)

This song showcases Stevie Ray Vaughan's incredible guitar skills. It is based on the 12-bar blues progression, a hallmark of his style.

••••••••••

These simple combinations of chords have worked for thousands of songs. Great artists who write or record others' songs have an ear for music, and much of it is based upon the fact that humans find simple chord progressions comforting and appealing. My dear old friend, *Billboard Multi-Platinum recording artist* **Glen Campbell**, said:

> *"Some people have said that I can 'hear' a hit song, meaning that I can tell the first time a song is played for me if it has potential. I have heard some hits that way, but I can also 'feel' one."*

When I was younger, I would hear hit songs on the radio and wonder how a song I felt wasn't as good as my originals ever became a hit in the first place. As I matured, I realized that every hit song has a bit of magic in it. It could be a repetitive line or a hook, a beautiful melody, or even a rap line you cannot get out of your head. Always look for an element of magic in your music!

Glen Campbell performing with Tad Sisler
Source – Sisler Private Collection

SIMPLE ACCOMPANIMENT PATTERNS

When I was six years old, my mother taught me how to use the "swing bass" with my left hand on the piano, establishing a rhythm for what I was playing by first playing the root note of a chord with my left hand, and then playing the chord itself in a rhythmic pattern. It was an excellent way to learn how to strengthen the coordination of my left hand. The right hand always seems to be the most coordinated of our two hands, so this was a good exercise.

For beginner pianists, mastering simple accompaniment patterns like block chords, broken chords, arpeggios, strumming patterns on keyboards with guitar sounds, and left-hand techniques provides a strong foundation for more complex playing and helps develop coordination and musicality.

BLOCK CHORDS involve playing all the notes of a chord simultaneously. This technique creates a solid sound and is straightforward for beginners to learn.
Example: In C major, a block chord would include C (root), E (major third), and G (perfect fifth) played together.
Start with simple triads (three-note chords) and practice transitioning between different chords smoothly.

BROKEN CHORDS, or arpeggios, are chords played with each note sounded separately rather than simultaneously. This technique adds movement and fluidity to the accompaniment.
Example: In C major, play C (root), E (major third), and G (perfect fifth) in sequence rather than together.
Practice broken chords slowly to ensure evenness and gradually increase the speed as you become more comfortable.

ARPEGGIOS are an extension of broken chords, where the notes of a chord are played in succession, often spanning multiple octaves. They can be played ascending or descending.

Example: In C major, an ascending arpeggio would be C (root), E (major third), G (perfect fifth), and C (octave).

Use a metronome to maintain a steady tempo and practice with both hands separately before combining them.

STRUMMING PATTERNS (FOR KEYBOARDS WITH GUITAR SOUNDS)

Strumming patterns on keyboards simulate the sound of a guitar being strummed. This action can add rhythmic interest and a different texture to your accompaniment.

Example: Using a keyboard's guitar sound, play a down-up-down-up pattern, mimicking the strumming motion of a guitar.

Start with simple downstrokes on the beat and gradually introduce upstrokes to create a more complex strumming pattern. When I was developing music for Yamaha keyboards, I got good at mimicking the guitar as it was played on the original recording. Now, on gigs, I can emulate a guitar closely with my technique on keyboard.

LEFT-HAND ACCOMPANIMENT TECHNIQUES

The left hand often provides the harmonic foundation and rhythmic support in piano playing. Common techniques include playing root notes, octaves, and simple bass lines.

Example: In C major, play the root note C or alternate between C and G (fifth) to create a bass line.

Start with simple patterns, such as playing root notes on the downbeat, and gradually introduce more complex rhythms and intervals. My mother taught a 'swing bass' pattern for left hand to establish rhythm on certain songs.

"I mean, give me a guitar, give me a piano, give me a broom and string, I wouldn't get bored anywhere!" – Keith Richards

Keith Richards
Credit – Wikimedia Commons

SECTION THREE
SIMPLE MELODIES

Now that we've explored chords, let's move on to playing simple single-note melodies:

FINGER TECHNIQUE

Proper Hand Position: Maintain a relaxed hand position with naturally curved fingers and keep your wrists level with the keyboard.

Finger Numbering: Use the correct finger numbers to ensure smooth transitions between notes. Thumb is 1, index finger is 2, your middle finger is 3, your ring finger is 4, and pinky finger is 5.

Smooth Transitions: Practice playing legato (smoothly connected) notes to create fluid melodies. Ensure each finger presses the keys with equal strength and clarity.

READING MELODIES FROM SHEET MUSIC

Excellent resources exist online for learning sheet music, including **MusicTheory.net** and **PianoNanny.com.** *Yamaha* has an extensive music teaching website.

Staff and Clefs: Familiarize yourself with the staff, treble clef, and bass clef. The treble clef signifies higher-pitched notes (right hand), and the bass clef is for lower-pitched notes (left hand).

Note Names and Values: Learn the names and values of notes. Practice identifying notes on the staff and corresponding keys on the piano.

Practice with Simple Pieces: Start with simple sheet music with single-note melodies. Focus on accuracy and rhythm.

EAR TRAINING EXERCISES: Ear training comes easy for some and hard for others. Here are a handful of tricks to help you along:

Interval Recognition: Practice recognizing intervals (the distance between two notes). Start with simple intervals like seconds, thirds, and fifths.

Melodic Dictation: Listen to simple melodies and try to play them by ear. Start with short, familiar tunes and gradually progress to more complex melodies.

Singing Notes: Sing the notes you play on the piano to reinforce pitch recognition and improve your musical ear.

CIRCLE OF FIFTHS

Take the time to learn the circle of fifths. Learning this helps you with theory, key signatures, chord progressions, and scale patterns:

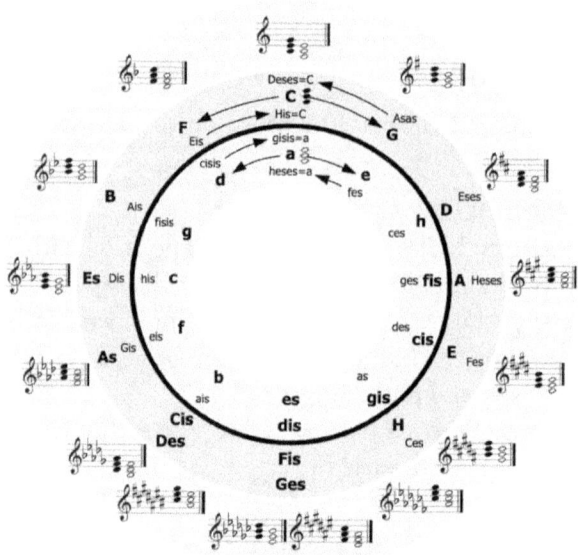

Circle of Fifths
Credit – Wikimedia Commons

Key Signatures: The circle of fifths visually shows you the relationship between different key signatures, making identifying sharps and flats in any key easier, helping you adapt quickly to different songs and genres.

Chord Progressions: Many common chord progressions in music follow the circle of fifths, such as I-IV-V or ii-V-I, helping you to anticipate chord changes and create more effective bass lines.

Improvisation: The circle of fifths helps you understand which chords and scales work well together, making it easier to improvise and create melodic bass lines that fit harmonically within a song.

Transposing: Knowing the circle of fifths helps you to transpose songs into different keys when you perform with other musicians or adapt to vocal ranges.

THREE EXAMPLES OF SONGS TO PRACTICE
"Twinkle, Twinkle, Little Star"
It is a classic children's song with a simple melody, ideal for beginners.
"Mary Had a Little Lamb"
It's another easy-to-play song with a repetitive melody.
"Ode to Joy" by Beethoven
A simple melody from Beethoven's Symphony No. 9, suitable for beginners.

PRACTICING WITH BACKGROUND TRACKS can help beginners maintain a steady rhythm and enhance their sense of timing. Look for tracks that match the songs you are learning. Utilize apps and websites that provide backing tracks for practice. Sites like **YouTube, Ultimate Guitar**, and **Piano Marvel** offer a variety of tracks for different skill levels. Start with a metronome to keep a consistent tempo before transitioning to full backing tracks.

"I think it's such a powerful thing: Words and melodies, and you put them together. I couldn't really picture a world without music. It would be quite boring." — Sabrina Carpenter

Sabrina Carpenter
Credit – Wikimedia Commons

USING BOTH HANDS - COORDINATING LEFT AND RIGHT HANDS

Hand Placement: Begin by placing your right hand in the middle C position and your left hand an octave below.

Practice Separately: Practice each hand separately to ensure you understand the notes and rhythm. Focus on getting comfortable with the individual parts before combining them.

Slow Practice: Start slowly when combining both hands. Increase the tempo as you become more comfortable. This exercise helps in developing coordination and timing.

SIMPLE TWO-HAND EXERCISES

Five-Finger Scales: Practice playing five-finger scales (C-D-E-F-G) with both hands simultaneously. This exercise helps develop basic coordination and finger strength.

Simple Chords: Play simple chords with the left hand while playing a melody with the right hand. Start with block chords (e.g., C major chord) and progress to more complex patterns.

Parallel Motion: Practice scales or simple melodies in parallel motion, where both hands move in the same direction and play the same notes an octave apart.

BASIC HAND INDEPENDENCE DRILLS

Contrary Motion Scales: Play scales with both hands moving in opposite directions. For example, start both hands on middle C, with the right hand ascending and the left hand descending.

Rhythmic Independence: Practice playing different rhythms with each hand. For instance, play quarter notes with the right hand while playing half notes with the left hand.

Simple Melodies and Chords: Play a simple melody with the right hand and basic chords or bass notes with the left hand. This exercise helps develop the ability to play independent parts with each hand.

THREE SONGS - PRACTICE USING BOTH HANDS

"Canon in D" by Johann Pachelbel

A simplified version of this classical piece is excellent for beginners. It helps in practicing coordination between both hands and understanding basic chord progressions.

"Fur Elise" by Ludwig van Beethoven

This famous piano piece has a recognizable melody that is satisfying to play. It involves simple arpeggios and chord progressions, making it perfect for beginners.

"Clair de Lune" bu Claud Debussy (Simplified Version)

A simplified arrangement of this beautiful piece can introduce beginners to expressive playing and hand coordination.

TIPS FOR SMOOTH TRANSITIONS

Slow Down: Practice transitions slowly to ensure accuracy and smoothness. Gradually increase speed as you gain confidence.

Spot Practice: Focus on the problematic parts of a piece, practicing them repeatedly until they become smooth.

Hand Shifts: Practice shifting hand positions smoothly by visualizing the new position and moving your hand confidently.

Consistent Practice: Regular practice helps build muscle memory, making transitions smoother over time.

DYNAMICS AND EXPRESSION

In the early days of computer music, programming, expression, and dynamics were not built as well into keyboards and drum machines as they are today. As a result, much of what we recorded could sound robotic. The human element makes music breathe, and it all starts with dynamics and expression.

PLAYING SOFTLY AND LOUDLY

Piano (p): Indicates to play softly. To achieve this, use a gentle touch on the keys.

Think about using the weight of your fingers rather than pressing down hard.

Forte (f): Indicates to play loudly. This requires more force and energy from your fingers and arms. Make sure to maintain control to avoid harshness.

Crescendo (cresc.): Gradually increase the volume.

Decrescendo (decresc.) or Diminuendo (dim.): Gradually decrease the volume.

USING THE SUSTAIN PEDAL

Learn to use the sustain pedal effortlessly, ensuring that each chord or phrase you play is sustained for just the right time and does not "bleed" into another chord or phrase. The sustain pedal (right pedal) lets notes ring out even after the keys are released, creating a smooth and connected sound. Press down the pedal with the ball of your foot. Release and press down again when changing chords to avoid blending notes inappropriately. Sometimes I'll drive many miles to a gig, and then perform for hours. Between the gas pedal and the sustain pedal, I've developed a huge muscle on my right calf!

ARTICULATIONS

Staccato (.): Play the note short and detached. To achieve this, quickly release the key after pressing it.

Legato (–): Play the notes smoothly and connected. Ensure that each note transitions to the next without any gaps.

Tenuto (–): Indicates that a note should be held for its full value or slightly longer, with emphasis. This articulation adds weight and significance to the note.

Accent (>): Indicates that a note should be played louder or with more force than the surrounding notes, adding emphasis.

Marcato (^): Indicates that a note should be played with strong emphasis and a slight detachment, combining elements of an accent and staccato.

Sforzando (sfz): Indicates a sudden, strong accent on a note or chord. It is often used to create dramatic emphasis.

Fermata (⌢): Indicates that a note or rest should be held longer than its usual duration, usually until the performer decides to continue.
It is used to add expressive pause or emphasis.

EXPRESSIVE PLAYING TECHNIQUES

Rubato: Slightly speeding up and slowing down the tempo for expressive effect. Use this technique sparingly to add emotional depth to the piece.

Phrasing: Think of the music in terms of sentences or phrases. Play each phrase with a sense of direction, leading to a natural ebb and flow in the music.

Remember, learning to play precisely and fast is essential, but speed is only part of the equation. Remember the words of the great pianist **Yuja Wang**

"It's not about how fast you can play. It's about what you say."

PIECES TO PRACTICE FOR EXPRESSION
"Moonlight Sonata" (First Movement) by Ludwig van Beethoven
Expressive phrasing, use of dynamics, and legato technique.
"Gymnopédie No. I" by Erik Satie
Soft dynamics, use of the sustain pedal, and expressive phrasing.
"Prelude in C Major" by Johann Sebastian Bach
Smooth legato playing, use of dynamics, and control of the sustain pedal.

Now that you're comfortable with the basics, let's move on to more challenging techniques.

CHAPTER THREE
INTERMEDIATE TECHNIQUES

EXPANDING YOUR REPERTOIRE
My friend, legendary broadcaster **Larry King** said:

"Basically, what it comes down to is I love what I do. I don't do it for fame. I don't do it for money. I just love it."

Larry King and Tad Sisler
Source – Sisler Personal Collection

My grandfather always said, *"If you're going to do a job, do it right, or don't do it at all."* Doing a job right includes learning the basics, becoming comfortable with the task at hand, and learning to love what you do. Embrace the experience of learning the piano, relax into the challenges and early frustrations, and do it for all the right reasons, and you are bound to succeed.

SECTION ONE
INTERMEDIATE CHORDS AND PROGRESSIONS
SEVENTH CHORDS AND BEYOND

DOMINANT SEVENTH (V7): A dominant seventh chord contains a root, major third, perfect fifth, and minor seventh. It is commonly used in classical and popular music to create a sense of tension that resolves to the tonic chord.

An example in C Major is G (root), B (major third), D (perfect fifth), and F (minor seventh)—written as G7.

Dominant seventh chords are used extensively in cadences and progressions, especially in blues, jazz, and classical music.

MAJOR SEVENTH (Maj7): A major seventh chord contains a root, major third, perfect fifth, and major seventh. It has a dreamy and relaxed sound.

An example in C Major is C (root), E (major third), G (perfect fifth), and B (major seventh)—written as Cmaj7.

Major seventh chords are often found in jazz, pop, and ballads, providing a smooth, lush sound.

MINOR SEVENTH (m7): A minor seventh chord contains a root, minor third, perfect fifth, and minor seventh. It has a rich, warm sound commonly used in jazz and blues.

Example in C Minor: C (root), Eb(minor third), G (perfect fifth), Bb(minor seventh) - written as Cm7.

Minor seventh chords are versatile and appear in various genres, adding depth and complexity to the music.

DIMINISHED SEVENTH (dim7): A diminished seventh chord contains a root, minor third, diminished fifth, and diminished seventh. It has a tense, dissonant sound.

Example in C Diminished: C (root), Eb (minor third), Gb (diminished fifth), Bbb (diminished seventh) - written as Cdim7.

Diminished seventh chords are often used in classical music and jazz to create tension and resolve to more stable chords.

PRACTICE EXERCISES

BUILDING SEVENTH CHORDS: Practice building dominant, major, minor, and diminished seventh chords starting from different root notes. Ensure you can quickly identify and construct each type of seventh chord.

Example: Play G7, Cmaj7, Fm7, Bdim7.

INVERSIONS: Practice playing seventh chords in different inversions to become familiar with their shapes and sounds. For example, take a Cmaj7 chord and play it in the root position, first inversion, second inversion, and third inversion.

Example: Cmaj7 - E-G-B-C, G-B-C-E, B-C-E-G.

Progressions: Practice common chord progressions that use seventh chords, such as ii-V-I. This exercise helps in understanding their role within a musical context.

Example in C Major: Dm7 (ii) - G7 (V) - Cmaj7 (I).

CHORD SUBSTITUTIONS: Experiment with substituting seventh chords instead of triads in familiar songs to hear how they alter the harmonic texture.

Example: Replace G with G7 in a simple progression like C - F - G - C.

Arpeggios: Play arpeggios of seventh chords to improve finger strength and fluidity.

Example: Cmaj7 arpeggio - C-E-G-B-E-G-B-C.

Seventh chords, including dominant seventh, major seventh, minor seventh, and diminished seventh, along with building exercises, chord substitution, and arpeggios, add depth and complexity to the music.

These lessons are giving you a lot to think about! Remember what my friend, *Billboard Multiple-Platinum* recording artist **Kenny Rogers**, said:

"I've always said music should make you laugh, make you cry, or make you think."

Tad Sisler and Family with Kenny Rogers
Source — Sisler Private Collection

ADVANCED CHORD PROGRESSIONS
JAZZ PROGRESSIONS

ii-V-I Progression: A staple in jazz, this progression involves moving from the ii chord to the V chord and resolving to the I chord.

Example in C Major: Dm7 (ii) - G7 (V) - Cmaj7 (I)

Creates smooth, harmonic resolutions and is foundational in many jazz standards.

I-VI-II-V Progression: Often used in jazz turnarounds and standard progressions.
Example in C Major: Cmaj7 (I) - A7 (VI) - Dm7 (II) - G7 (V)
Adds a sense of movement and return within the piece.

COLTRANE CHANGES
A complex series of chord changes popularized by **John Coltrane**, often involving modulations by major thirds.
Example: Cmaj7 - Ab7 - Dbmaj7 - Emaj7 - G7
Used for rapid harmonic shifts and creating tension.

Alice Coltrane, the widow of legendary saxophonist **John Coltrane**, was a master pianist. She fluidly played piano, organ, and harp, and her unique style incorporated elements of spiritual jazz, gospel, Indian classical music, and avant-garde jazz.

Alice Coltrane
Credit – Wikimedia Commons

POP PROGRESSIONS
I-V-vi-IV Progression: Known as the "Axis of Awesome" progression, it is widely used in pop music.
Example in C Major: C (I) - G (V) - Am (vi) - F (IV)
Creates a catchy and familiar sound used in many pop hits.

IV-V-I Progression: A familiar cadence in pop and rock music.
Example in C Major: F (IV) - G (V) - C (I)
Provides a strong resolution and is often used at the end of phrases.
vi-IV-I-V Progression: Another popular progression in pop music.
Example in C Major: Am (vi) - F (IV) - C (I) - G (V)
Frequently used in choruses and verses for its pleasing resolution.

CLASSICAL PROGRESSIONS
I-IV-V-I Progression: A fundamental progression in classical music, creating a strong sense of resolution.
Example in C Major: C (I) - F (IV) - G (V) - C (I)

Common in cadences and harmonic structures.

I-vi-IV-V Progression: Used in many classical compositions, providing a pleasing harmonic progression.

Example in C Major: C (I) - Am (vi) - F (IV) - G (V)

Creates a balanced and harmonious sound.

I-V-vi-iii-IV-I-IV-V Progression: Often found in classical pieces, providing a rich harmonic landscape.

Example in C Major: C (I) - G (V) - Am (vi) - Em (iii) - F (IV) - C (I) - F (IV) - G (V)

Adds complexity and variety to classical compositions.

THREE SONGS TO PRACTICE

"Take the A Train" by Duke Ellington (Jazz):

Progression: Various jazz changes, including ii-V-I

It is a jazz standard with rich harmonic progressions.

"Someone Like You" by Adele (Pop):

Progression: I-V-vi-IV

It's a contemporary pop song with a classic progression.

"Minuet in G Major" by Johann Sebastian Bach (Classical)

Progression: This piece uses a variety of classical progressions, including I-IV-V-I and more complex sequences.

The more advanced you become, the more you feel like you are making magic. **Billy Joel** and I met at my gig in La Jolla, California, a handful of years back. He was cool to hang out with and very supportive. We talked about the magic of playing the piano. **Billy Joel** famously said:

"In a way, we are magicians. We are alchemists, sorcerers, and wizards. We are a very strange bunch, but there is great fun in being a wizard."

Billy Joel
Credit — Wikimedia Commons

INCORPORATING MODES

A mode is a musical scale with a specific pattern of whole and half steps, creating distinct tonalities and moods.

MAJOR MODES

Ionian Mode: This is the same as the major scale. It consists of whole and half steps in the following order: W-W-H-W-W-W-H.
Example: C-Ionian (C-D-E-F-G-A-B-C)
Lydian Mode: Similar to the major scale but with a raised fourth. The sequence is: W-W-W-H-W-W-H.
Example: C-Lydian (C-D-E-F#-G-A-B-C)
Mixolydian Mode: Like the major scale but with a lowered seventh. The sequence is: W-W-H-W-W-H-W.
Example: C-Mixolydian (C-D-E-F-G-A-Bb-C)

MINOR MODES

Aeolian Mode: Natural minor scale.
The sequence is: W-H-W-W-H-W-W.
Example: A-Aeolian (A-B-C-D-E-F-G-A)
Dorian Mode: Like the natural minor scale but with a raised sixth. The sequence is W-H-W-W-W-H-W.
Example: D-Dorian (D-E-F-G-A-B-C-D)
Phrygian Mode: Like the natural minor scale but with a lowered second. The sequence is: H-W-W-W-H-W-W.
Example: E-Phrygian (E-F-G-A-B-C-D-E)

MODAL INTERCHANGE (or modal mixture) involves borrowing chords from parallel modes (modes that share the same tonic). For example, in the C major key, you can borrow chords from C minor modes (C Aeolian, C Dorian, C Phrygian).
Example: In C major, you can use chords like C minor (Cm), E flat major (Eb), and A flat major (Ab), which are borrowed from C minor modes.

THREE SONGS TO PRACTICE

"So What" by Miles Davis
Mode: D Dorian - A classic example of modal jazz, it uses the Dorian mode extensively.

"Norwegian Wood" by The Beatles
Mode: Mixolydian - This song features the Mixolydian mode, giving it a unique sound.

"Eleanor Rigby" by The Beatles
Mode: Aeolian - It uses the natural minor scale to create a somber and reflective mood.

IMPROVISATION WITH MODES

Understand the Mode: Familiarize yourself with the notes and the characteristic intervals of the mode you are using. Practice scales and arpeggios within that mode.

Chord Tones and Tensions: Focus on the underlying harmony's chord tones and use the mode's characteristic notes to create tension and resolution.

Phrase Development: Develop your phrases by starting with simple motifs and expanding them. Use repetition, sequence, and variation.

Rhythmic Variation: Experiment with different rhythms to add interest to your improvisation. Syncopation, rests, and varying note lengths can create compelling solos.

Practice Backing Tracks: Use backing tracks to practice modal improvisation. This addition helps develop the ability to navigate the mode over different harmonic contexts.

SECTION TWO
ADVANCED FINGER EXERCISES AND SCALES
FINGER INDEPENDENCE EXERCISES

Next, we'll get into the 'weeds' of working on coordination. Practice and repetition are the keys to excellent piano performance. A few good resources exist online, as well as physical workbooks and tutorials to help you learn **Hanon Exercises** and **Czerny Studies**.

BENEFITS OF FINGER INDEPENDENCE

Improved Dexterity: Enhanced ability to play complex passages with speed and accuracy.

Increased Control: Greater control over dynamics and articulation, leading to more expressive playing.

Balanced Technique: More even and balanced technique across all fingers, preventing over-reliance on stronger fingers.

Reduced Strain: Better finger independence minimizes the risk of strain and injury by promoting proper technique.

Enhanced Musicality: The ability to play independent lines with each hand, crucial for contrapuntal music and advanced pieces.

HANON EXERCISES

The **Hanon** exercises from *"The Virtuoso Pianist in 60 Exercises"* by **Charles-Louis Hanon** are designed to improve finger strength, dexterity, and independence. They involve repetitive patterns that focus on different finger combinations. I spent countless hours poring through the **Hanon** books when I was learning, and the lessons were extremely valuable to me. Although this can be tedious, it increased my passion for performing as I improved.

Example: *Exercise No. 1* focuses on repeated patterns using all five fingers. Practice these exercises daily, starting slowly and gradually increasing speed as accuracy and comfort improve.

The **Righteous Brothers** duo **Bill Medley** and **Bobby Hatfield** recorded the single most played song on American Radio during the 20th century, *"You've Lost that Lovin' Feelin'."* Part of **Phil Spector's** *Wall of Sound*, they went on to record many other hits during their extensive career. Since **Hatfield** passed away in 2003, **Medley** has continued performing well into the 21st Century. My friend **Bill Medley** said:

"Passion: It's what separates a singer from an entertainer. I hope I have a passion for my music, my family, and my friends until they start shovelling dirt on my face."

Tad Sisler with the Righteous Brothers
Source – Sisler Private Collection

CZERNY STUDIES
Carl Czerny's studies, particularly from *"The School of Velocity"* and *"The Art of Finger Dexterity,"* focus on developing technical skills and finger independence through various musical patterns and scales.
Example: Op. 299, No. 1 involves rapid note patterns that require each finger to act independently. Incorporate Czerny studies into your daily practice routine to develop technical proficiency and finger independence.

CUSTOM EXERCISES
Tailor exercises to address specific finger weaknesses and improve overall dexterity. Custom exercises can include scales, arpeggios, and specific finger patterns.
Example: Create an exercise focusing on playing scales with only the 3rd and 4th fingers, which are often weaker and less independent.
Develop a variety of custom exercises targeting different finger combinations and incorporate them into your practice routine.

DAILY PRACTICE ROUTINES

Warm-Up: Begin with simple finger exercises and scales to warm up the fingers.

Technical Exercises: Spend 15-20 minutes on **Hanon** and **Czerny** exercises, focusing on accuracy and evenness.

Custom Exercises: Integrate custom exercises that target specific finger independence issues.

Repertoire Practice: Apply the techniques developed in exercises to your repertoire, ensuring that finger independence translates to musical pieces.

Cool-Down: End with light, relaxing exercises to cool down the fingers.

ADVANCED SCALE PATTERNS

Every great pianist has spent countless hours playing scales. Learning scales helps a jazz or pop performer solo over different chord changes and improves dexterity and coordination.

HARMONIC MINOR SCALE: This is a natural scale in minor with a raised seventh degree, giving it a distinctive sound, often associated with classical and Eastern music.

Pattern: W-H-W-W-H-W+H-H (Whole note, Half note, Whole, Whole, Half, Whole and a Half, Half)

Example in A Minor: A-B-C-D-E-F-G#-A

MELODIC MINOR SCALE: The melodic minor scale differs in its ascending and descending forms. Ascending, it raises the sixth and seventh degrees; descending, it goes back to the natural minor scale.

Pattern Ascending: W-H-W-W-W-W-H

Pattern Descending: W-W-H-W-W-H-W (same as the natural minor)

Example in A Minor (Ascending): A-B-C-D-E-F#-G#-A

Example in A Minor (Descending): A-G-F-E-D-C-B-A

WHOLE TONE SCALE: The whole tone scale is made up entirely of whole steps, resulting in a very symmetrical and ambiguous sound, often used in Impressionist music.

Pattern: W-W-W-W-W-W

Example in C: C-D-E-F#-G#-A#-C

DIMINISHED SCALE: The diminished scale, or the octatonic scale, alternates whole and half steps. There are two types: the half-whole diminished scale and the whole-half diminished scale.

Pattern (Half-Whole): H-W-H-W-H-W-H-W

Pattern (Whole-Half): W-H-W-H-W-H-W-H

Example (Half-Whole in C): C-Db-Eb-E-F#-G-A-Bb-C

Example (Whole-Half in C): C-D-Eb-F-Gb-Ab-A-B-C

I've mentioned that, in many ways, music is mathematics. Navigating your way through any genre demands proficiency, coordination, and expressiveness. Legendary trumpeter **Wynton Marsalis said** it this way:

"Swing is extreme coordination. It's about maintaining balance and equilibrium. It's about executing very difficult rhythms with panache and a feeling in the context of very strict time. So, everything about the swing is about some guideline and some grid and the elegant way that you negotiate your way through that grid."

Wynton Marsalis
Credit – Wikimedia Commons

SCALE PRACTICE TECHNIQUES

Hands Separately and Together: Practice scales with each hand separately before combining them. This exercise ensures each hand can perform the scale independently.

Slow Practice: Start slowly to ensure the accuracy and evenness of notes. Gradually increase the tempo as you become more comfortable.

Varied Rhythms: Practice scales in different rhythmic patterns (e.g., dotted rhythms, triplets) to develop flexibility and control.

Dynamic Variation: Play scales with varying dynamics, such as crescendo (gradually getting louder) and decrescendo (getting progressively softer).

Articulations: Practice scales using different articulations, such as legato (smooth and connected), staccato (short and detached), and accents.

Inversions and Octaves: Practice scales in different octaves and with various inversions to improve finger independence and familiarity with the keyboard layout.

"It seems like I always had to work harder than other people. Those nights when everybody else is asleep, and you sit in your room trying to play scales." - B.B. King

B.B. King
Credit – Wikimedia Commons

PRACTICING ARPEGGIOS

Arpeggios are fun and dynamic. The great pianist **Liberace** was the king of arpeggios. I met him in Palm Springs, California, when I was raising my kids. We went to the same grocery store. Later, I performed private parties and corporate events at his house on his piano with the famous candelabras.

Nowadays, any sequencing keyboard can play arpeggios independently, but learning how to play them yourself is still essential.

MAJOR ARPEGGIOS: A major arpeggio consists of the root, major third, and perfect fifth of a major chord, played sequentially.

Example in C Major: C-E-G

Play hands separately before combining. Use a metronome to maintain tempo. Start slowly and gradually increase speed.

MINOR ARPEGGIOS: A minor arpeggio consists of the root, minor third, and perfect fifth of a minor chord, played in sequence.

Example in A Minor: A-C-E

Focus on the evenness of each note. Practice hands separately and together. Use fingerings that promote smooth transitions.

INVERSIONS: Inversions of arpeggios involve playing the notes of the arpeggio in different orders. Each inversion starts with a different note of the chord.

First Inversion: The third is the lowest note.

•Example in C Major: E-G-C

•**Second Inversion**: The lowest note: Fifth

•Example in C Major: G-C-E

Practice each inversion separately. Ensure smooth transitions between notes in each inversion. Combine inversions with root position to create fluid arpeggio patterns.

BROKEN ARPEGGIOS: Broken arpeggios involve playing the notes of the arpeggio in a non-linear, non-sequential pattern.

Example in C Major: C-G-E, G-E-C, E-C-G

Experiment with different patterns of breaking the arpeggio. Practice hands separately before combining. Use broken arpeggios to add variety to your practice routine.

THREE PRACTICE PIECES

"Clocks" by Coldplay

This is a modern rock song that incorporates repetitive arpeggio patterns in the piano part, creating a driving and rhythmic feel.

Practice Focus: Repetitive arpeggio patterns and maintaining rhythmic consistency.

"Piano Sonata No. 16 in C Major, K. 545" by Wolfgang Amadeus Mozart

Often referred to as the "Sonata facile" or "Easy Sonata," this piece includes arpeggiated patterns that are accessible yet elegant, making it a staple for intermediate pianists.

Practice Focus: Clarity and precision in arpeggio patterns, light touch, and classical phrasing.

"Jesu, Joy of Man's Desiring" by Johann Sebastian Bach (Arranged for Piano)

This arrangement of Bach's choral piece includes arpeggiated accompaniments that create a beautiful, flowing texture.

Practice Focus: Smooth, legato arpeggios, maintaining a steady rhythm, and expressive phrasing.

I always encourage piano students to learn songs they want to play, like contemporary popular songs, especially at first when you need to stay motivated through the hard part. In the same breath, I feel just as passionate about encouraging learning classical music.

Nobody said it better than **Snoop Dogg**:

"You've got to always go back in time if you want to move forward."

Keep an open mind to learning every genre you can... which leads me to my next section...

Snoop Dogg and Tad Sisler
Source – Sisler Private Collection

SECTION THREE
BUILDING A DIVERSE REPERTOIRE
LEARNING PIECES FROM DIFFERENT GENRES

Learning pieces from different genres involves understanding each genre's unique characteristics and techniques. You can develop skills and versatility by focusing on specific practice tips, allowing you to perform many musical styles with confidence and expressiveness.

CLASSICAL PIECES: Classical music emphasizes precision, technique, and expressive interpretation. Start with sight-reading to familiarize yourself with the notes and structure. Practice hands separately to master complex passages. Use a metronome to practice slowly, gradually increasing the tempo. Pay close attention to dynamics and articulation marks. Work on phrasing and musicality to bring out the expressive qualities of the piece. I've released a dozen albums of classical piano music. It's exhilarating to play, but I would have to practice constantly to perform it live. Classical piano can be hard work!

JAZZ STANDARDS: Jazz music focuses on improvisation, swing rhythm, and complex harmonies. Learn and practice various jazz chord voicings. Practice improvisation using scales and modes, such as the **Dorian** and **Mixolydian** modes. Focus on mastering the swing rhythm and syncopation. Transcribe solos from famous jazz recordings to understand stylistic nuances. Develop your ear, recognizing chord changes and melodic lines. I've enjoyed the releases of jazz standards I've recorded and performed over the years. The melodies of the Great American Song Book will last for generations.

So very many jazz pianists have shaped how we approach our jazz performances. My favorites are **Oscar Peterson, George Shearing, McCoy Tyner,** and **Bud Powell.** Jazz took a different turn when pianists like **Keith Jarrett, Ahmad Jamal, Bill Evans, Chick Corea,** and **Herbie Hancock** reinvented the approach. All are worthy of studying and appreciating.

Oscar Peterson
Credit – Flickr/Creativecommons.org

POPULAR SONGS: Pop music features catchy melodies, simple chord progressions, and a strong focus on rhythm. Learn common pop chord progressions (e.g., I-V-vi-IV). Focus on maintaining a steady rhythm and groove. Pay attention to the melody and how it fits with the lyrics. Practice different accompaniment patterns, such as block chords and arpeggios. Sing along or practice with backing tracks to simulate performance conditions.

ROCK MUSIC often features powerful chords, strong rhythms, and energetic performances. Practice playing power chords and rock chord progressions. Work on precise rhythm and timing. Use dynamics to add intensity and variation to your playing. Transcribe and learn solos from famous rock songs. Practice with a focus on energy and stage presence. Rock music is a blast to play!

BLUES MUSIC features the blues scale, expressive bends, and a strong sense of rhythm and groove. Learn and practice the blues scale in various keys. Master the 12-bar blues progression. Practice call-and-response phrasing. Work on improvising with the blues scale and pentatonic scale. Focus on the feel and groove, making your playing sound authentic. There's nothing more exhilarating than great blues piano.

COUNTRY MUSIC often features storytelling, simple chord progressions, and a focus on melody. Practice open chords and simple chord progressions. Develop fingerpicking techniques for accompaniment. Focus on the narrative aspect of the lyrics. Learn common country rhythmic patterns. Emphasize clear and melodic playing.

REGGAE features offbeat rhythms, syncopation, and a laid-back groove. Focus on playing offbeat rhythms with precision. Practice syncopated rhythmic patterns. Develop a strong sense of groove and feel. Learn common reggae chord progressions. Incorporate bass lines into your playing to create a fuller sound.

NEW AGE PIANO is a genre that emphasizes soothing, atmospheric compositions, often characterized by gentle melodies, repetitive motifs, and a peaceful, meditative quality. It blends elements of classical, jazz, and minimalism with modern sensibilities to create relaxing and reflective music that is frequently used for meditation, yoga, and relaxation. The genre became especially popular in the 1980s and 1990s, with artists focusing on creating ambient, emotionally evocative soundscapes. Three popular New Age piano artists include **George Winston**, known for his seasonal albums like *Autumn*, **David Lanz**, whose compositions often feature lush, melodic themes, and **Yanni**, whose blend of piano and synthesizers helped bring New Age music to a wider audience. I tried my hand at a New Age album with my *"Watching the Wind"* release, a handful of years back:

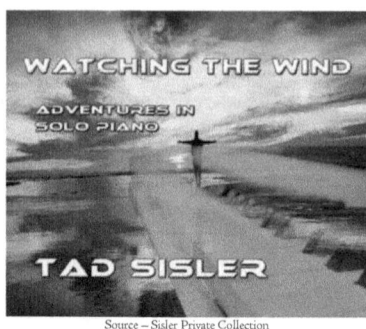

WORLD MUSIC encompasses a variety of musical styles from different cultures, including African, Indian, Middle Eastern, and Latin American music. Learn and practice unique rhythmic patterns from different cultures. Study scales and modes used in world music, such as the Raga scales in Indian music or the pentatonic scales in African music. Understand the role of different instruments and how to incorporate their sounds into your playing. Practice improvisation within the context of different world music styles. Listen to a wide variety of world music to understand different styles and techniques.

Great things happen in our lives by chance or by design. We learn to play the piano and keyboards through design, and then we discover new elements of ourselves through chance or serendipity in the process. Nobody understood that more than my friend, MULTI-PLATINUM artist **Sergio Mendes**, an icon of Latin popular music.

There's a word in the English language that I like, "Serendipity"; it's the story of my life." – Sergio Mendes

Sergio Mendes and Tad Sisler

TECHNIQUES FOR MEMORIZING MUSIC

I can play almost three thousand songs. I could possibly be in the *Guinness Book of World Records* if I stopped and played them back-to-back over a period. I'm not exactly sure how the human brain works to retain so much music, but it amazes me, after ten years, how a song comes back to me. I know part of it is because of endless repetition through the years and because I learned or created some techniques to help myself remember music and lyrics. I'm not an aberration or necessarily unique in this manner. I believe that anyone can train themselves through memory exercises. Here are a handful of exercises that may work for you:

CHUNKING involves breaking down the music into smaller, manageable sections or "chunks" and memorizing each individually. Break the piece into small sections, such as phrases, measures, or thematic units. Concentrate on memorizing one chunk at a time. Gradually connect the chunks to form larger sections of the piece. **Chunking** helps to prevent feeling overwhelmed by the entire piece and makes the memorization process more systematic.

VISUALIZATION involves imagining the keyboard, hand movements, and the sound of the music in your mind without physically playing it. Close your eyes and visualize playing the piece, including finger positions and movements. Imagine the sound of each note and the overall flow of the piece. Picture the sheet music in your mind and mentally follow along. **Visualization** enhances muscle memory and internalizes the music, making it easier to recall during performance.

REPETITION is the process of playing a passage multiple times to reinforce memory. Focus on small sections and repeat them until you memorize them. Use varied repetitions by changing dynamics, tempo, or articulation to deepen memory. Include regular, spaced repetitions over multiple practice sessions. **Repetition** reinforces neural pathways, making the music more ingrained and easier to recall.

PLAYING BY EAR involves learning and memorizing music by listening rather than reading sheet music. Listen to recordings of the piece multiple times. Familiarize yourself with the melody, harmony, and rhythm. Sing or hum the melody to internalize it. Try to play the piece by ear, starting with the melody and gradually adding harmony. Connecting sound with finger movements enhances aural skills, deepens understanding of the music, and aids in memorization.

MEMORY RETENTION EXERCISES

Practice sections of the piece starting from the end and working backward. Memorize each hand separately before combining them. Test your memory by playing the piece without looking at the sheet music and identify sections where memory lapses occur. Alternate between practicing different sections or pieces to improve memory retention. Away from the piano, try to recall and visualize playing the piece mentally. **This exercise enhances** cognitive flexibility, strengthens neural connections, and improves overall memory retention.

Memorizing becomes easier through practice. My good friend, *Major League Baseball Hall of Fame* Pitcher **Trevor Hoffman,** said:

"When you routinely do the things you have to do to get ready, everything does become second nature."

Prepare. Believe in the process. Believe in yourself.

Tad Sisler with Trevor Hoffman
Source – Sisler Private Collection

PERFORMING FOR OTHERS

I was frightened beyond belief when I went to walk into my first full-time gig. I sat in my car in the parking lot, praying for the strength and confidence to face other people. I would be surprised if you don't have a fraction of fear or self-doubt about performing. Here are some tips:

OVERCOMING STAGE FRIGHT

Accept that nervousness is normal and can be channelled into positive energy. Thorough preparation can increase confidence. Before the actual performance, practice performing in front of friends or family. Use deep breathing exercises to calm your nerves before and during the performance. Visualize a successful performance. Imagine yourself playing confidently and the audience enjoying your music. Concentrate on the music rather than how you are perceived. This action shifts attention away from self-doubt.

PREPARING FOR PERFORMANCES

Develop a regular practice routine to build muscle memory and familiarity with the piece. Simulate the performance environment by playing through the entire piece without stopping, as you would in an actual performance. Test your memory by playing sections of the piece that are out of order and away from the piano. On the performance day, do a proper warm-up to ensure your fingers are agile and responsive. Get adequate rest and eat a balanced meal before the performance to ensure you are physically and mentally prepared.

ENGAGING THE AUDIENCE

Make brief eye contact with the audience before and after your performance to create a connection. Use confident and expressive body language to convey emotions and engage the audience. Briefly introduce the piece or share a personal story related to the music to draw the audience in. Focus on expressive playing and dynamics to captivate the audience's attention. Acknowledge the audience's applause with a smile and a bow at the end of your performance.

FEEDBACK AND IMPROVEMENT

After the performance, ask for feedback from teachers, peers, or audience members to gain insights into areas of improvement. Record your performances to self-assess and identify strengths and weaknesses. Reflect on the feedback and your observations to create an improvement plan. Focus on specific areas highlighted during feedback in your practice sessions. View feedback as a tool for growth and improvement and maintain a positive mindset.

PERFORMANCE OPPORTUNITIES

Recitals: Participate in student recitals organized by your teacher or music school.

Competitions: Enter local or national piano competitions to gain experience and exposure.

Community Events: Perform at community centers, nursing homes, or local events to gain confidence and share your music.

Online Performances: Use social media platforms to share your performances and connect with a broader audience.

Collaborations: Collaborate with other musicians for ensemble performances or chamber music. Performing on an advanced level comes down to one word: Practice!

CHAPTER FOUR
ADVANCED TECHNIQUES AND IMPROVISATION

Improvisation in different music genres allowed artists like **Miles Davis** in jazz to create spontaneous compositions, **Jimi Hendrix** in rock to deliver electrifying solos, and **Bob Marley** in reggae to infuse rhythmic variations, showcasing their unique styles and enhancing live performances.

"To be a good improviser, you have to study composition as a parallel. Because what improvisation is, on a high level, is spontaneous composition." – Roscoe Mitchell

Roscoe Mitchell
Credit – Wikimedia Commons

SECTION ONE
COMPLEX CHORD VOICINGS

Learning complex chord voicings, including extended and altered chords, chord substitutions, and related practice exercises, enriches a pianist's harmonic vocabulary and enhances their ability to create sophisticated and expressive music.

EXTENDED CHORDS include notes beyond the basic triad (root, third, fifth) and seventh chords, such as the ninth, eleventh, and thirteenth.
Example: Cmaj9 (C-E-G-B-D), C13 (C-E-G-Bb-D-A)
Application: Commonly used in jazz, gospel, and R&B to add richness and colour.
Inversions: Practice playing extended chords in different inversions.
Voice Leading: Focus on smooth transitions between extended chords by practicing voice leading.
Arpeggios: Play extended chords as arpeggios to familiarize your fingers with the spacing and sound.

ALTERED CHORDS contain one or more altered notes, such as a sharpened or flattened fifth, ninth, or eleventh.
Example: G7#9 (G-B-D-F-A#), G7b13 (G-B-D-F-Eb)
Application: Frequently used in jazz to create tension and resolve.
Altered Scale Practice: Practice scales that include altered notes to improve your familiarity with these tones.
Resolving Tensions: To understand their function, practice resolving altered chords to their target chords (e.g., G7#9 to Cmaj7).
Voice Leading: Work on smooth voice leading when transitioning from altered chords to other chord types.

CHORD SUBSTITUTIONS involve replacing a chord with another with a similar harmonic function but adds variety and complexity.

Example: Using a tritone substitution, such as replacing G7 with Db7 in a ii-V-I progression (Dm7—Db7—Cmaj7).

Application: Commonly used in jazz and contemporary music to add harmonic interest.

Tritone Substitution: Practice tritone substitutions in various keys and progressions.

Related ii-V Substitution: Substitute ii-V pairs with their related ii-V counterparts.

Diatonic Substitution: Practice substituting diatonic chords within a key to explore different harmonic possibilities.

PRACTICE EXERCISES

Chord Voicing Drills:

Play extended and altered chords in all inversions.

Use a metronome to practice smooth transitions between voicings.

Progression Practice:

Practice ii-V-I progressions with extended and altered chords.

Incorporate chord substitutions into common progressions (e.g., ii-V-I, I-vi-ii-V).

Arpeggios and Scales:

Practice arpeggios of extended and altered chords.

Play scales corresponding to extended and altered chords to understand their harmonic context.

Voice Leading:

Practice smooth voice leading between complex chords.

Focus on maintaining common tones and moving other voices by step.

HOW TO APPLY VOICINGS IN DIFFERENT GENRES

Jazz Standards:

Incorporate extended and altered chords into jazz standards like "Autumn Leaves" or "All the Things You Are."

Pop and Contemporary Music

Use chord substitutions and extended chords to add complexity to pop songs.

Classical Music:

Apply advanced voicings in contemporary classical compositions or arrangements.

Blues and R&B:

Enhance blues progressions with extended and altered chords for a richer sound.

On several occasions, I performed for my old friend, **President Gerald R. Ford**. A few times, I performed before he spoke to an audience, and he always had me play the *Michigan Fight Song* while he was walking onstage.

Long before he was President, he played football in college in Michigan and told me that hearing the song emboldened him to give a strong speech. **President Ford** said:

"When a man is asked to make a speech, the first thing he has to decide is what to say."

Piano performance is like public speaking in this manner. Every tool in your arsenal gives you the voice to tell your musical story your way.

President Gerald R. Ford and Tad Sisler
Source – Sisler Private Collection

ADVANCED RHYTHM AND TIMING: A sarcastic saying about drummers is, *"So many drummers, so little time."* I've performed with the greatest drummers on the planet with impeccable timing. Mastering advanced rhythm and timing techniques is crucial for pianists aiming to enhance their musicality and versatility, develop a deeper understanding of rhythm, improve their timing, and add expressiveness to their playing. Plus, there's no greater joy than knowing how to play in the pocket!

POLYRHYTHMS involve playing two or more contrasting rhythms simultaneously. A typical example is playing three notes in one hand against two in the other (3:2 polyrhythm). Begin with simple polyrhythms like 2:3 or 3:4. Clap the rhythms separately, then together, to internalize the feel. Practice the rhythms with each hand separately before combining. Use a metronome to practice slowly, ensuring accuracy before increasing speed.

SYNCOPATION involves placing emphasis on weak or off-beats, creating rhythmic variety and complexity. Start with simple syncopated patterns and gradually increase complexity. Count out loud to understand where the syncopation falls within the measure. Metronome use helps to maintain a steady beat while practicing syncopation. Subdivide the beats to grasp the timing of syncopated notes better.

ARTIST SPOTLIGHT
NINA SIMONE

Nina Simone was an American pianist, singer and songwriter pioneering her own blend of jazz, blues, and classical music. She broke the color barrier in music and dedicated her life to social causes. About her style, **Nina** said:

> *"I wasn't a jazz player, but a classical musician, and I improvised arrangements of popular songs using classical motifs."*

Remember to always think innovation while you're learning progressions in different genres, much like **Nina** did.

Nina Simone
Credit – Roland Godefroy – Wikimedia Commons

RUBATO, meaning "stolen time," involves the flexible adjustment of tempo for expressive purposes, slowing down or speeding up as the music demands. Focus on the emotional content of the piece and how rubato can enhance it. Make small, slight changes in tempo rather than large, abrupt ones. Maintain an underlying sense of pulse, even while varying the tempo. Work with a teacher or compare your playing to recordings to develop a nuanced sense of rubato.

GROOVE, also known as playing in the pocket, refers to the sense of rhythmic feel or "swing" that makes the music compelling and danceable. It's essential in genres like jazz, funk, and pop. Listen to music recordings with solid grooves and try to imitate the feel. Practice with a metronome set to different subdivisions (e.g., eighth notes, triplets) to internalize different rhythmic feels. Engage your body by tapping your foot or swaying to the beat to embody the groove. Focus on maintaining a consistent and steady groove throughout your practice. **Herbie Hancock** and **George Duke** are two of my favorite groove keyboardists.

EXPRESSIVE PLAYING TECHNIQUES

DYNAMIC CONTROL involves varying the volume of your playing to convey emotion and create contrast within a piece. Dynamics range from very soft (pianissimo) to thunderous (fortissimo). Practice scales and arpeggios at different dynamic levels, gradually increasing or decreasing the volume. Practice pieces that include crescendos (gradually getting louder) and decrescendos (gradually getting softer) to develop control over dynamic transitions. Emphasize specific notes with accents to highlight key moments in the music.

VIBRATO: While vibrato is more commonly associated with string instruments, pianists can emulate a vibrato effect by using rapid, subtle oscillations in pitch or volume. This technique can be used for expressive effects, particularly in slower, lyrical passages. Practice trills (rapid alternation between two adjacent notes) and tremolos (rapid repetition of a single note or chord) to develop the finger strength and control needed for vibrato-like effects. Apply subtle vibrato techniques in pieces that require emotional depth.

GLISSANDO: A glissando is a rapid slide up or down the keyboard, creating a cascading effect of notes. This technique is often used for dramatic effect. Use the back of your fingers (usually the third or fourth finger) to slide smoothly across the keys. Practice glissandos slowly at first to develop control and avoid injury. Keep your hand relaxed and slightly curved to facilitate a smooth glide across the keys.

PEDAL TECHNIQUES
The piano has three pedals—soft (una corda), sostenuto, and sustain (damper)—each used to enhance expressiveness differently.
Soft Pedal (Una Corda): Softens the sound and alters the tone color.
Sostenuto Pedal: Sustains only the notes being played when the pedal is pressed, allowing for selective sustaining.
Sustain Pedal (Damper): Lifts all the dampers off the strings, allowing all notes to ring out and blend together.
Sustain Pedal: Practice pressing and releasing the sustain pedal in coordination with your playing to create smooth legato lines.
Una Corda: Use the soft pedal for passages that require a gentler, more intimate sound.
Sostenuto Pedal: Experiment with the Sostenuto pedal in pieces that require holding specific notes while playing others staccato or detached.

PRACTICE PIECES FOR EXPRESSIVE PLAYING
"Rhapsody in Blue" by George Gershwin
Focus: Executing glissandos effectively and adding drama to the performance.
"Nocturne in E-flat Major, Op. 9, No. 2" by Frédéric Chopin
Focus: Using the sustain pedal to create smooth legato lines and exploring dynamic nuances.
"La Campanella" by Franz Liszt
Focus: Dynamic control and rapid, delicate passages. This piece requires precise articulation and expressive dynamic changes. Focus on creating clear, bell-like tones and maintaining dynamic contrast throughout.

SECTION TWO
INTRODUCTION TO IMPROVISATION

"With improvisation, I just do it. It might be a total failure but then you just throw the dice again." — Christian Marclay

Christian Marclay
Credit — Wikimedia Commons

BASIC IMPROVISATION TECHNIQUES

Basic improvisation techniques for pianists include:
- Using scales and modes.
- Creating and developing motifs.
- Constructing phrases.
- Practicing with various exercises.

Regular practice and experimentation with these elements will lead to greater confidence and proficiency in improvisation.

SCALES AND MODES

Major and Minor Scales: Fundamental to improvisation, major and minor scales provide the basic building blocks for melodies and harmonies.

Example: C Major Scale (C-D-E-F-G-A-B-C), A Minor Scale (A-B-C-D-E-F-G-A)

Pentatonic Scales: Five-note scales that are easy to use and pleasing in many contexts.

Example: C Major Pentatonic (C-D-E-G-A)

Blues Scale: Adds a bluesy feel to improvisation, incorporating flattened notes.

Example: C Blues Scale (C-Eb-F-Gb-G-Bb-C)

Modes: Different modes offer unique flavors derived from the major scale, starting on different scale degrees.

Example: Dorian Mode (D-E-F-G-A-B-C-D), Mixolydian Mode (G-A-B-C-D-E-F-G)

CREATING MOTIFS

A motif is a short, recurring musical idea or theme that can be developed throughout an improvisation. Repeat the motif in different contexts or registers. Alter the rhythm, intervals, or dynamics of the motif. Transpose the motif up or down the scale. Flip the motif so ascending intervals become descending and vice versa.

DEVELOPING PHRASES

A phrase is a longer musical idea, often made up of several motifs. Create a conversational structure between phrases. Extend the motif by adding new material at the end. Introduce new material to contrast with the initial motif. One phrase poses a musical question, and the following phrase provides the answer.

PRACTICE EXERCISES

Play scales and modes in different keys and practice improvising simple melodies using these scales.

Motif Creation: Create a short motif and practice developing it using repetition, variation, sequencing, and inversion.

Call and Response: Practice call-and-response improvisation with a recording or a fellow musician.

Phrase Development: Extend a simple melody by adding new phrases, contrasting ideas, and question-and-answer structures.

Chord Progressions: Improvise over common chord progressions, such as I-IV-V, ii-V-I, or blues progressions.

SIMPLE IMPROVISATION PIECES

"Autumn Leaves" (Jazz Standard)

Focus on improvising over the ii-V-I progression and incorporating motifs and phrases.

"Watermelon Man" by Herbie Hancock

Use blues scales and pentatonic scales to improvise over the funky groove.

"Summertime" by George Gershwin

Practice modal improvisation using the Dorian mode.

"I always say that improvisation is the utterance of one's spirit, and it dictates your life experience, and that's how you find your concepts and your way for painting your musical picture." – Dianne Reeves

Dianne Reeves
Credit – Wikimedia Commons

IMPROVISATION IN DIFFERENT GENRES

JAZZ: Jazz improvisation emphasizes creativity, complex harmonies, and spontaneous expression. It often involves modal and chromatic scales, syncopation, and intricate chord progressions.

Learn Jazz Standards: Familiarize yourself with common jazz standards and their chord progressions.

Chord Voicings: Practice different chord voicings and extensions (e.g., 9ths, 11ths, 13ths).

Modal Improvisation: Use modes such as Dorian, Mixolydian, and Lydian for soloing.

Transcription: Transcribe solos from jazz legends to understand their phrasing and techniques.

Rhythmic Variation: Experiment with different rhythms and syncopations to add interest to your improvisations.

BLUES: Blues improvisation focuses on emotional expression.
It uses the blues scale, pentatonic scales, and call-and-response patterns and typically follows a 12-bar blues progression.

Blues Scale: Practice the blues scale in various keys.

12-Bar Blues: Familiarize yourself with the 12-bar blues progression.

Bending and Sliding: Incorporate note bending and sliding techniques to add expressiveness.

Call and Response: Practice call-and-response phrasing within your solos.

Feel and Groove: Focus on the groove and feel of the blues, making your improvisation sound authentic.

CLASSICAL: Classical improvisation involves ornamentation, embellishment, and thematic development, often within the stylistic constraints of the Baroque, Classical, or Romantic periods.

Ornamentation: Practice trills, mordents, and other ornaments typical of classical music.

Cadenzas: Study and practice cadenzas from concertos and other works.

Theme and Variation: Develop variations on a theme, a common practice in classical improvisation.

Historical Context: Understand the stylistic conventions of the period you're improvising in.

Structured Improvisation: Follow the structure and form typical of classical compositions.

POP: Pop improvisation emphasizes catchy melodies, simple chord progressions, and rhythmic consistency. It often involves playing over familiar chord changes and adding personal flair.

Chord Progressions: Practice common pop chord progressions (e.g., I-V-vi-IV).

Melodic Hooks: Focus on creating memorable melodic hooks in your improvisation.

Rhythmic Patterns: Experiment with different rhythmic patterns to add interest.

Sing Along: Practice singing your improvised lines to develop a solid melodic sense.

Playback and Record: Record your improvisations and play them back to identify areas for improvement.

REGGAE: Reggae improvisation focuses on offbeat rhythms, syncopation, and a laid-back groove.
It often incorporates simple melodic lines and rhythmic variations.

Offbeat Accents: Practice playing chords and melodies with offbeat accents.

Syncopation: Incorporate syncopated rhythms into your improvisation.

Simple Melodies: Focus on simple, catchy melodies that fit the reggae groove.

Bass Lines: Practice creating reggae-style bass lines with your left hand while improvising with your right hand.

Listening: Listen to reggae music to internalize the groove and feel.

LATIN MUSIC: Latin music improvisation involves complex rhythms, syncopation, and specific scales and modes. It encompasses styles like salsa, bossa nova, and tango.

Clave Rhythms: Practice the clave rhythms fundamental to many Latin styles.

Latin Scales: Use scales like the harmonic minor and Phrygian mode in your improvisation.

Rhythmic Patterns: Incorporate common Latin rhythmic patterns such as montuno and tumbao.

Percussive Elements: Add percussive elements to your playing, such as hitting the piano keys with a rhythmic touch.

Listening and Transcription: Listen to and transcribe solos from Latin jazz musicians to understand their phrasing and techniques.

USING BACKGROUND TRACKS

Many online resources exist to find great backing tracks for any purpose. Assuming you set up a great practice space as we already outlined, you should improvise over background tracks, record your improvisations, and analyse your performances for fluidity and sophistication. Remember, as with anything, practice makes perfect. Just think how blessed you are to be using this magnificent gift of talent! I always keep in mind the words of my friend, legendary actor **Robert Wagner**:

"I've learned one important thing about God's gifts — what we do with them is our gift to him."

Robert Wagner and Tad Sisler
Source – Sisler Private Collection

SECTION THREE
ADVANCED MUSIC THEORY

UNDERSTANDING HARMONIC FUNCTIONS

TONIC: The tonic is the home chord of a key and provides a sense of resolution and stability. It is the I chord in major and minor keys.

Example: In C major, the tonic chord is C major (C-E-G).

Tonic chords establish the key and often appear at the beginning and end of phrases or pieces to create a sense of closure.

DOMINANT: The dominant chord creates tension that resolves to the tonic. It is the V chord in a key and often includes a seventh to increase tension.

Example: In C major, the dominant chord is G major (G-B-D) or G7 (G-B-D-F).

Dominant chords lead to the tonic, creating a sense of movement and resolution. They are crucial in cadences and chord progressions.

SUBDOMINANT: The subdominant chord, the IV chord in a key, provides a sense of preparation and movement towards the dominant.

Example: In C major, the subdominant chord is F major (F-A-C).

Subdominant chords are often used to move away from the tonic and towards the dominant, creating a smooth progression flow.

SECONDARY DOMINANTS: Secondary dominants are dominant chords that temporarily tonicize a chord other than the tonic. They add interest and complexity to progressions.

Example: In C major, the secondary dominant of D minor (ii) is A7 (A-C#-E-G), leading to D minor.

Secondary dominants are used to create temporary modulations and add harmonic variety.

MODULATION: Modulation is when you change from one key to another within a piece. It can be smooth (diatonic modulation) or abrupt (chromatic modulation).

Example: Modulating from C major to G major using a D7 chord (V of G) to lead into G major.

Modulation creates contrast, maintains interest, and develops musical ideas. Common modulations include moving to the dominant or relative minor/major.

PRACTICE EXERCISES

Analyze simple pieces and identify tonic, dominant, and subdominant chords. Practice labeling secondary dominants and modulation points in sheet music. Practice common progressions like I-IV-V-I, ii-V-I, and I-vi-ii-V in different keys. Include secondary dominants in your practice (e.g., I-V/ii-ii-V-I). Improvise melodies over a progression using tonic, subdominant, and dominant chords. Experiment with secondary dominants and modulations in your improvisations. Practice smooth voice leading between chords, focusing on familiar tones and stepwise motion.

APPLICATION IN MUSIC

Classical: In classical music, harmonic functions create structured, balanced compositions. Tonic, dominant, and subdominant chords define the form and cadence points.

Jazz: Jazz musicians use harmonic functions to navigate chord changes and improvisation. Secondary dominants and modulations are common in jazz standards.

Pop and Rock: Pop and rock songs often use simple progressions (I-IV-V). Still, they can include secondary dominants and modulations for added interest. **Barry Manilow** was the king of modulating one step higher into another key to add excitement towards the end of his songs.

Blues: The 12-bar blues progression relies heavily on tonic, subdominant, and dominant chords.

Film and Game Music:

Modulations and secondary dominants create dramatic shifts and maintain interest in more extended compositions.

EXPLORING COUNTERPOINT

"To me it's no accident that all the symphony orchestras around the world tune up to the note A. And A is 440 cycles, except in Germany where it's 444. But the universe is 450 cycles. So what I'm trying to say is, I think it's Gods voice, melody especially. Counterpoint, retrograde inversion, harmony... that's the science and the craft." — Quincy Jones

Quincy Jones
Credit – Wikimedia Commons

Understanding counterpoint involves:
•Writing independent yet harmonically interdependent melodies.
•Practicing with pieces that exemplify contrapuntal techniques.
•Analyzing classical works.
•Applying these concepts in modern music.

WRITING SIMPLE COUNTERPOINT

Counterpoint is the relationship between two or more independent melodies that are harmonically interdependent but independent in rhythm and contour.
First Species: Note against note.
Second Species: Two notes against one.
Third Species: Four notes against one.
Fourth Species: Syncopation, involving tied notes.
Fifth Species: Florid counterpoint, combining all species.

COUNTERPOINT IN TWO POPULAR SONGS

"God Only Knows" by The Beach Boys: This classic song from the album PET SOUNDS features intricate vocal harmonies and counterpoint. The intertwining melodies of the voices create a rich and complex texture, making it a standout example of counterpoint in popular music. Each vocal line is distinct yet harmoniously blends with the others, demonstrating the band's sophisticated arrangement skills.
"Scarborough Fair/Canticle" by Simon & Garfunkel: In this song, Simon & Garfunkel overlay the traditional folk melody of "Scarborough Fair" with a counter-melody called "Canticle." The two distinct melodies, sung simultaneously, create a haunting and beautiful counterpoint. The juxtaposition

of the melodies and their thematic contrasts enhance the song's depth and complexity, showcasing the duo's mastery of counterpoint techniques.

STEPS FOR WRITING COUNTERPOINT

Start with a Cantus Firmus: Begin with a simple, singable melody in one voice.

Add a Contrapuntal Voice: Write a second melody that fits harmonically and rhythmically with the cantus firmus.

First Species: Write one note for each note of the cantus firmus, ensuring consonance (unison, third, fifth, sixth, octave).

Second Species: Write two notes for each note of the cantus firmus, maintaining consonance on strong beats and allowing passing tones on weak beats.

Third Species: Write four notes for each note of the cantus firmus, using passing tones, neighbor tones, and other non-harmonic tones.

Fourth Species: Use syncopation and tied notes to create suspensions and resolve dissonances.

Fifth Species: Combine elements from all previous species for a more elaborate and flowing texture.

PRACTICE PIECES

"Fugue in C Minor, BWV 847" from The Well-Tempered Clavier by Johann Sebastian Bach: Complex counterpoint with multiple voices.

"Ave Maria" by Josquin des Prez: Vocal counterpoint adapted for piano, illustrating polyphonic texture.

"Canon in D" by Johann Pachelbel: Canonical imitation and voice independence.

Hélène Grimaud is a French classical pianist with profound emotional depth and poetic interpretations of great classical works. She feels strongly that any work can be elevated by the artists interpretation. **Hélène** said:

> *"Music does not live until it's interpreted — with all of its flaws, mannerisms, etc. It needs to be incarnated to be something."*

Hélène Grimaud
Credit – Wikimedia Commons

MAKE A DIFFERENCE WITH YOUR BOOK REVIEW
Unlock the Power of Generosity
"The joy of giving lasts longer than the joy of receiving."

Back when I worked as a developer for *Yamaha,* I learned from the very best about how to make music sound full and alive on a keyboard, as close to a real performance as possible. Working with keyboards and pianos and with countless other musicians taught me so much about how to make music and share it with others. Now, I want to share that with you, whether you're just starting or reaching for a new level with piano or keyboard.

Would you help someone just like you—curious about playing piano and keyboards but not sure where to start?

My mission is to make piano playing easy, successful, rewarding, and fun for everyone.

But to reach more people, I need your help.

Most people choose books based on reviews. So, I'm asking you to help another pianist by leaving a review.

It doesn't cost anything and takes less than a minute, but it could change someone's musical journey. Your review could help...

- ...one more person find their passion for music.
- ...one more child discover the joy of playing.
- ...one more student feel confident in learning.
- ...one more dream come true.

If you purchased my book on Amazon, here's the link to leave your review:

https://www.amazon.com/review/review-your-purchases/?asin=196625802X

Or you can just scan this QR code to get to the Amazon review page:

If you love helping others, you're my kind of person. Thank you from the bottom of my heart!   **Tad Sisler**

ANALYZING CLASSICAL WORKS
"Fugue in G Minor, BWV 578" by Johann Sebastian Bach
Identify the subject, countersubject, and episodes. Note how Bach develops each voice and uses inversion, augmentation, and diminution.

"Missa Papae Marcelli" by Giovanni Pierluigi da Palestrina: Examine the use of counterpoint in a choral setting, focusing on the interaction between voices and the use of consonance and dissonance.

APPLYING COUNTERPOINT IN MODERN MUSIC

Jazz: Use counterpoint in jazz by creating independent melodic lines within a chord progression. Artists like **Dave Brubeck** and **Bill Evans** incorporate contrapuntal techniques.

Exercise: Improvise two independent melodies over a standard jazz progression, ensuring harmonic coherence.

Pop and Rock: Introduce counterpoint in vocal harmonies or instrumental lines. Bands like **The Beatles** and **Queen** often use contrapuntal techniques.

Exercise: Write a simple pop melody and add a second voice that creates harmonic interest and rhythmic independence.

Film and Game Music: Counterpoint creates texture and complexity in soundtracks. Composers like **John Williams** and **Nobuo Uematsu** employ counterpoint to enhance emotional impact.

Exercise: Compose a short piece for a film or game scene using multiple independent melodic lines to create tension and resolution.

"The most immediately gratifying thing about my work is conducting a large orchestra. But the long-range payoff is composing because you've written something and it's there forever." – Henry Mancini

COMPOSITION TECHNIQUES for pianists involve creating themes, developing motifs, structuring compositions, understanding orchestration basics, and practicing various exercises. Regular practice and experimentation with these elements will lead to greater proficiency and creativity in composition.

CREATING THEMES: A theme is a central, recurring melody or idea that forms the basis of a composition. Start with a simple, memorable melody that can be easily recognized and developed. Focus on the shape of the melody, using stepwise motion and leaps for interest. Establish a distinct rhythmic pattern to make the theme stand out. Use basic chords (I, IV, V) to support the theme and create a strong harmonic underpinning.

DEVELOPING MOTIFS: A motif is a short, recurring musical idea or fragment that can be developed throughout a composition. Repeat the motif to establish it in the listener's mind. Alter the motif by changing its rhythm, intervals, or dynamics. Transpose the motif up or down the scale to create a sequence. Flip the motif so ascending intervals become descending and vice versa. Increase or decrease the note values of the motif.

STRUCTURING A COMPOSITION involves organizing musical ideas into a coherent form.
Binary Form (AB): Two contrasting sections, often repeated (AABB).
Ternary Form (ABA): Three sections, with the first and third being identical or similar, and the middle section contrasting.
Sonata Form: Consists of an exposition (introducing themes), development (exploring and varying themes), and recapitulation (returning to the original themes).
Rondo Form (ABACA): A principal theme alternates with contrasting episodes.
Through-Composed: Continuous, non-repetitive music without a structured form.

BASICS FOR ORCHESTRATION
Orchestration involves arranging a composition for different instruments, considering their unique timbres and ranges. Understand the characteristics and roles of strings, woodwinds, brass, and percussion. Distribute melodies, harmonies, and rhythms across different instruments to create a balanced and rich texture. Use multiple instruments to play the same part for a fuller sound. Combine contrasting timbres to highlight different sections and create interest. Use dynamic markings and articulation to enhance expressiveness.

COMPOSITION EXERCISES
Theme Creation: Write a simple 8-bar melody focusing on melodic contour and rhythmic identity.
Motif Development: Create a 2-bar motif and develop it using repetition, variation, sequence, and inversion.
Form Practice: Compose a short piece in binary (AB) or ternary (ABA) form.
Orchestration: Arrange a simple piano piece for a small ensemble (string quartet or woodwind trio).

Harmonic Exploration: Write a chord progression and create a melody over it. Experiment with different harmonizations and modulations.

APPLICATION IN MUSIC

Classical: Use thematic development and structured forms like sonata or rondo to create cohesive compositions.

Jazz: Incorporate motifs and variations in improvisation and composition. Explore different forms like AABA or blues.

Pop and Rock: Focus on catchy themes and uncomplicated forms (verse-chorus). Use orchestration to enhance recordings.

Film and Game Music: Use thematic development to create memorable leitmotifs. Orchestrate to match the mood and setting of scenes.

Too many genres exist to explore them all, so within the next chapter, we will focus on the most popular genres for pianists and keyboardists. Take the time to explore music worldwide, and you'll find that many of the techniques we've outlined translate to other forms of music.

CHAPTER FIVE
EXPLORING DIFFERENT MUSICAL GENRES

W herever you're from or whatever influences you, remember that all music is expression, and every genre contains magic. One of the great blessings of my life was my friendship with *National Football League* Hall-of-Fame Linebacker **Junior Seau**. **Junior** spoke of his influences in his own way by saying:

"As I was coming up, it always seemed like I was learning.
If it wasn't from school, it was the 'hood.'
The influences of the 'hood' are very powerful."

Tad Sisler and Junior Seau
Source – Sisler Private Collection

Remember, as we explore a handful of genres, that versatility is the key to becoming well-rounded.

SECTION ONE
CLASSICAL PIANO

CLASSICAL COMPOSERS

JOHANN SEBASTIAN BACH: **Bach** is renowned for his intricate and masterful use of counterpoint, and his works are considered the pinnacle of Baroque music.
Practice Piece: "Prelude in C Major, BWV 846" from The Well-Tempered Clavier.

LUDWIG VAN BEETHOVEN: **Beethoven's** compositions bridge the Classical and Romantic eras, characterized by their emotional depth and innovative structures.
Practice Piece: "Für Elise".

WOLFGANG AMADEUS MOZART: **Mozart's** music is celebrated for its clarity, balanced form, and lyrical melodies, which epitomize the classical style.
Practice Piece: "Sonata in C Major, K. 545".

FREDERIC CHOPIN:: **Chopin's** compositions are primarily for solo piano and are marked by their expressive depth and innovative use of piano technique.
Practice Piece: "Prelude in E Minor, Op. 28, No. 4".

FRANZ SCHUBERT:: **Schubert** is known for his melodic inventiveness and rich harmonic language, bridging the Classical and Romantic periods with his lieder and symphonic works.
Practice Piece: "Impromptu in G-flat Major, Op. 90, No. 3".

CLASSICAL TECHNIQUES AND STYLES

BAROQUE: Baroque music (1600-1750) is characterized by intricate counterpoint, ornamentation, and the use of the harpsichord. Composers like **J.S. Bach** and **Handel** are prominent figures in this style. Practice scales, arpeggios, and exercises like **Hanon** to develop finger independence and dexterity. Focus on accurately executing trills, mordents, and other ornaments. Practice pieces with multiple voices separately before combining them to understand the interplay between lines.

CLASSICAL: Classical music (1750-1820) emphasizes clarity, balanced form, and expressive melody. Composers like **Mozart, Haydn**, and early **Beethoven** are key figures. Develop a clear and even touch, avoiding heavy pedalling to maintain clarity. Focus on creating lyrical, singing phrases and observing dynamic markings. Understand the formal structures, such as sonata-allegro form, to guide your interpretation.

ROMANTIC: Romantic music (1820-1900) is characterized by its emotional expressiveness, complex harmonies, and expansive forms. Key composers include **Chopin, Liszt, Schumann,** and later **Beethoven.** Emphasize expressive phrasing and dynamic contrast to convey the music's emotional depth. Practice using rubato to add expressiveness, ensuring it remains within the piece's style and context. Focus on overcoming technical challenges like rapid passages and wide leaps by practicing slowly and gradually increasing speed.

CONTEMPORARY CLASSICAL: Contemporary piano music (1900-present) encompasses many atonal, minimalistic, and experimental styles. Composers like **Debussy, Ravel, Prokofiev,** and **Philip Glass** are notable. Be open to exploring unconventional techniques and sounds, such as playing inside the piano or using a prepared piano (a piano that has altered sounds by placing screws, mutes, bolts, rubber erasers, or other objects on or between the strings). Focus on mastering complex rhythms and changing time signatures. Experiment with different touch and pedal techniques to explore a variety of tone colours and textures.

INTERPRETING CLASSICAL MUSIC involves:
- Understanding historical context.
- Adhering to performance practices.
- Conveying emotional expression.
- Utilizing dynamics and phrasing effectively.

HISTORICAL CONTEXT

Each era has its own stylistic conventions and aesthetic values.

Research: Study the composer's life, influences, and historical events during composition.

Compare Recordings: Listen to historically informed performances and modern interpretations to understand different approaches.

Hiromi Uehara (Hiromi) is a great example of an accomplished pianist who energetically blends jazz with classical, rock, fusion, and electronic influences, creating her own virtuosity, interpreted with impeccable technique.

Hiromi Uehara
Credit – Robert Drozd – Wikimedia Commons

PERFORMANCE PRACTICES

Different periods have unique performance practices, such as ornamentation in Baroque music or rubato in Romantic music.

Baroque: Incorporate ornamentation like trills and mordents and use a precise, detached touch.

Classical: Emphasize clarity, balance, and structured phrasing with minimal pedal use.

Romantic: Use expressive rubato and a wide dynamic range, focusing on emotional depth.

Contemporary: Be open to unconventional techniques and interpretive freedom.

EMOTIONAL EXPRESSION

Understanding the mood and character intended by the composer guides expressive choices. Identify the character and mood of different sections and adjust touch, tempo, and dynamics accordingly. Connect personally with the music to convey genuine emotion.

DYNAMICS AND PHRASING

Dynamics and phrasing bring music to life, adding shape and contrast to the performance. Follow dynamic markings and experiment with volume gradations to enhance expressiveness. Understand musical phrases' natural rise and fall and use breath-like pauses to shape them.

"The notes I handle no better than many pianists. But the pauses between the notes – ah, that is where the art resides!" – Artur Schnabel

ANALYSIS OF THREE FAMOUS PIECES

"Prelude in C Major, BWV 846" by Johann Sebastian Bach: Composed during the Baroque period, emphasizing intricate counterpoint.

Performance Practices: Use of ornamentation, even touch, and minimal pedal.

Emotional Expression: Convey a sense of calm and order through precise execution.

Dynamics and Phrasing: Maintain steady dynamics with subtle phrasing to highlight the harmonic progression.

"Sonata in C Major, K. 545" by Wolfgang Amadeus Mozart: Classical period, focusing on clarity and balance.

Performance Practices: Light touch, clear articulation, and limited pedal use.

Emotional Expression: Convey elegance and simplicity with a playful character in faster movements.

Dynamics and Phrasing: Use dynamics to highlight contrasts and shape phrases with clear beginnings and endings.

"Prelude in E Minor, Op. 28, No. 4" by Frédéric Chopin: Romantic period, emphasizing personal expression and lyrical beauty.
Performance Practices: Use of rubato, legato touch, and rich dynamics.
Emotional Expression: Convey deep introspection and sorrow with a flowing, cantabile style.
Dynamics and Phrasing: Gradual dynamic swells and phrasing reflect the ebb and flow of the melody.

SECTION TWO
JAZZ AND BLUES PIANO

JAZZ COMPOSERS AND ARTISTS
The following jazz composers/pianists significantly contributed to their respective genres, each bringing a unique style and voice to their music. Practicing pieces by these composers can help you develop a deeper understanding of jazz and blues idioms and improve your improvisational skills:

Duke Ellington
Credit: Library of Congress via Picryl.com

DUKE ELLINGTON: Duke Ellington was a pioneering jazz composer and bandleader known for his sophisticated orchestral arrangements and prolific output.
Practice Piece: "In a Sentimental Mood"
THELONIUS MONK: Thelonious Monk was a groundbreaking jazz pianist and composer whose unique improvisational style and innovative compositions have impacted jazz music.
Practice Piece: "Round Midnight"
COUNT BASIE: Count Basie was a legendary jazz pianist and bandleader whose minimalist piano style and swinging arrangements defined the sound of the Big Band era.
Practice Piece: "One O'Clock Jump"

SCOTT JOPLIN: Scott Joplin, the "King of Ragtime," was a seminal composer whose syncopated melodies and intricate rhythms helped define early American popular music.

Practice Piece: "Maple Leaf Rag"

RAY CHARLES: Ray Charles, "The Genius," highlighted in Chapter Six of this book, was a versatile musician whose fusion of blues, jazz, gospel, and R&B created a distinctive sound.

Practice Piece: "Georgia on My Mind"

KEY ELEMENTS OF JAZZ PIANO

SWING RHYTHM: Swing rhythm is characterized by a distinctive "long-short" pattern, in which the first note in a pair is held longer, and the second note is shorter, creating a "swinging" feel. Listen to classic swing recordings to internalize the feel. Practice playing eighth notes with a swung rhythm, focusing on the uneven timing.

IMPROVISATION: As we've already described, improvisation in jazz involves spontaneously creating melodies and harmonies within the framework of a song's chord changes and structure. Practice scales (e.g., major, minor, blues) and modes (e.g., Dorian, Mixolydian) in various keys. Transcribe solos from jazz greats to understand their improvisational techniques and phrasing.

JAZZ CHORDS: Jazz chords often include extensions (9ths, 11ths, 13ths) and alterations (b5, #5, b9, #9), providing richer harmonic textures. Learn and practice various jazz chord voicings, including rootless and drop-two. Practice common jazz progressions like ii-V-I in all keys, incorporating extended and altered chords.

BLUES COMPOSERS AND ARTISTS

Practicing pieces by these artists help pianists develop a deeper understanding of blues piano techniques and styles, enhancing their overall musicianship.

W.C. HANDY: **W.C. Handy**, the *"Father of the Blues,"* was a composer and musician who popularized the blues genre through his published works.

Practice Piece: "Beale Street Blues"

PINETOP PERKINS: **Pinetop Perkins** was a legendary blues pianist known for his energetic boogie-woogie style and as a member of the **Muddy Waters Band**.

Practice Piece: "Pinetop's Boogie Woogie"

OTIS SPANN: **Otis Spann** was a highly influential Chicago blues pianist renowned for his passionate playing and collaborations with **Muddy Waters**.

Practice Piece: "Otis in the Dark"

MEMPHIS SLIM: **Memphis Slim** was a prolific blues pianist and singer whose career spanned several decades. He was known for his sophisticated style and storytelling.
Practice Piece: "Lend Me Your Love"

Memphis Slim
Credit – Wikimedia Commons

PROFESSOR LONGHAIR: **Professor Longhair**, a cornerstone of New Orleans blues and R&B, was celebrated for his rhythmic complexity and unique piano style.
Practice Piece: "Tipitina"

BLUES TECHNIQUES

BLUES SCALE: A blues scale traditionally is a six-note scale that includes the root, minor third, fourth, diminished fifth (or sharp fourth), fifth, and minor seventh is a blues scale.
Example: C Blues Scale: C, Eb, F, F#, G, Bb
Practice the blues scale in different keys to build finger dexterity and familiarity. Use the blues scale to improvise over a 12-bar blues progression.

TWELVE-BAR BLUES: The twelve-bar blues is a chord progression that typically follows a specific pattern over twelve measures, using the I, IV, and V chords.
Example in C:
Measures 1-4: C (I)
Measures 5-6: F (IV)
Measures 7-8: C (I)
Measures 9: G (V)
Measures 10: F (IV)
Measures 11-12: C (I)
Practice the twelve-bar blues progression in all keys to gain versatility. Experiment with different left-hand accompaniment patterns, such as walking bass lines or boogie-woogie patterns.

RHYTHM AND BLUES (R&B): Rhythm and blues (R&B) blend elements of blues, jazz, and gospel music, characterized by its strong rhythm, soulful melodies, and use of blues scales and chords. Focus on developing a solid sense of groove and rhythm. Practice standard R&B chord voicings and progressions, emphasizing smooth transitions and soulful expression. Listen to classic R&B recordings to internalize the style and feel.

BOOGIE-WOOGIE: Boogie-woogie is a style of blues piano characterized by its fast tempo, repetitive left-hand patterns, and energetic right-hand improvisations. Whenever I play boogie-woogie in the bars and nightclubs, the audience wakes up! Master common boogie-woogie left-hand patterns, such as the walking bass and rolling eighth notes. Practice improvising over the left-hand patterns using blues scales and riffs. Focus on coordinating both hands, maintaining a steady left-hand rhythm while improvising with the right hand.

COMBINING JAZZ AND BLUES

"I'm this strange kind of fusion of jazz, pop, and R&B." – Al Jarreau

Al Jarreau
Credit – Wikimedia Commons

Fusion has many interpretations in jazz and blues music. Modern jazz fusion usually combines many styles, as illustrated by bands like **Weather Report, Snarky Puppy, and Hiromi's Sonicbloom**. Combining jazz and blues techniques involves blending both genres' improvisational approaches, rhythmic elements, and harmonic complexities. My friend **Joel Martin** is an amazing classical pianist. He "invented" a new style called **Jazzical,** where he incorporates classical and jazz elements together. Regular practice of these techniques and listening to and analysing fusion pieces will help pianists develop a versatile and expressive playing style that honors jazz and blues traditions.

INTERPRETATION TECHNIQUES
Blues Scale in Jazz Context: Use the blues scale to improvise over jazz chord progressions, blending the raw emotion of blues with the harmonic complexity

of jazz. Practice improvising over ii-V-I progressions using the blues scale alongside jazz modes like Dorian or Mixolydian.

Jazz Chords with Blues Feel: Incorporate jazz chords with extensions and alterations (e.g., 9ths, 11ths, 13ths) while maintaining a bluesy feel in your phrasing and expression. Practice playing jazz standards with a bluesy touch, emphasizing using blues notes and inflections.

RHYTHM AND GROOVE

Swing and Shuffle: Combine the swing rhythm of jazz with the shuffle rhythm of blues to create a dynamic and engaging groove. Alternate between swing and shuffle rhythms to develop versatility.

Syncopation: Syncopation adds rhythmic interest, blending jazz' off-beat accents with blues' steady groove. Practice syncopated rhythms in both hands, ensuring tight coordination and rhythmic accuracy.

PRACTICE EXERCISES

Blues Scales Over Jazz Progressions: Improvise using the blues scale over jazz progressions like ii-V-I, focusing on smooth transitions and blending styles.

Extended Chords in Blues: Incorporate extended jazz chords into traditional twelve-bar blues progressions, experimenting with different voicings.

Left-Hand Patterns: Practice boogie-woogie left-hand patterns while improvising jazz melodies with the right hand.

Transcription: Transcribe solos from jazz-blues fusion artists to understand their approach and phrasing.

LISTENING RECOMMENDATIONS

"Freddie Freeloader" by Miles Davis
Fusion Element: Combines the blues scale with jazz improvisation over a blues form.

"The Thrill Is Gone" by B.B. King
Fusion Element: Showcases blues guitar techniques with jazz-influenced phrasing and harmony.

"Blue Monk" by Thelonious Monk
Fusion Element: This is a jazz blues piece that highlights Monk's unique style and use of blues elements in a jazz context.

Contemporary Jazz and Smooth Jazz are sub-genres of Jazz, combining elements of R&B, Fusion, Rock, Easy Listening, and Jazz. Artists like **Joe Sample** and **David Benoit** paved new roads in piano styling with their sophisticated changes and arrangements. I was performing in a lounge in Palm Springs, California, several years ago and **Joe Sample** came in and sat at the bar. I was young and intimidated by his presence, so I stepped it up and attempted to play as many sophisticated jazz chords and arrangements as I could (as if I

92

could ever impress the master!). He looked up and smiled, and nodded a few times in appreciation, and that was enough for me!

SECTION THREE
POP AND ROCK KEYS
POP/ROCK ARTISTS
The following iconic pop and rock composers/pianists have significantly contributed to music with their unique styles and memorable compositions:

ELTON JOHN: **Elton John** was featured in Chapter One.
Practice Piece: "Rocket Man"
BILLY JOEL, often called the "Piano Man," is a celebrated multi-platinum singer-songwriter and pianist with storytelling lyrics and catchy melodies.
Practice Piece: "Uptown Girl"
CAROLE KING is a renowned singer-songwriter and pianist whose influential album *"Tapestry"* and numerous hits made her one of the most successful female artists in pop music history.
Practice Piece: "It's Too Late"
PAUL McCARTNEY, co-founder of **The Beatles**, is a multi-instrumentalist and singer whose innovative contributions to pop and rock music made him the most successful composer in music history.
Practice Piece: "Let It Be"
BRUCE HORNSBY is a versatile pianist and singer-songwriter known for his unique blend of rock, jazz, bluegrass, Americana and his impressive improvisational skills.
Practice Piece: "The Way It Is"

"When I have the time at home, I'll practice three or four hours a day. I have to. And I'm a late starter; I started at age 17 and at age 51 I'm still learning." – Bruce Hornsby

Bruce Hornsby
Credit – Creativecommons.org

KEY ELEMENTS OF POP KEYBOARD

You can enhance your skills and creativity as a pop and rock keyboardist by incorporating synthesis basics, programming sounds, and regular practice exercises into your routine.

CHORD PROGRESSIONS

Practice playing common pop progressions, including I-V-vi-IV and ii-V-I in various keys to gain fluency. Focus on smooth transitions between chords, using inversions to minimize hand movement.

SYNTHESIZERS

Experiment with different oscillators, filters, presets and parameters to understand how various sounds are created. Practice layering multiple sounds to create rich, textured tones.

ROCK KEYBOARD TECHNIQUES

Practice playing power chords in different positions on the keyboard, focusing on tight, clean execution. Learn and practice iconic rock riffs and licks to build a repertoire and improve finger dexterity.

SYNTH AND ELECTRONIC MUSIC

Synthesis involves creating sounds from scratch using oscillators, filters, envelopes, and LFOs (Low-Frequency Oscillators). Start with simple waveforms (sine, square, sawtooth) and experiment with modifying them using filters and envelopes. Use software synths or hardware to program custom sounds, focusing on understanding each parameter's effect on the overall sound.

PRACTICE EXERCISES

Practice common pop chord progressions in various keys, using both hands to play full chords and adding rhythmic variations. Spend time each day experimenting with synthesizer settings to create and save new sounds. Improvise over common chord progressions using riffs, licks, and synth sounds, focusing on developing your unique style.

I grew up in the modern age of music. As a performer, I've worked in every venue imaginable, from small smoky nightclubs to stadiums with thousands of people watching. My recording career has been just as varied.

From working on reel-to-reel 8-track machines in the early 1980s, then graduating to the 2-inch, 24-track systems in the larger studios, moving over to digital audio tape, and then to *Pro Tools* on hard drives, I've seen it all up to this point. Who knows what AI will bring in the coming years? When I started, we spliced tape and accidentally recorded over many outstanding performances by accident. Now, recording has become seamless and inexpensive. All you need is a little knowledge, and you can do it all, especially if you're a keyboardist.

CHAPTER SIX
PERFORMING AND RECORDING TECHNIQUES
ARTIST SPOTLIGHT
RAY CHARLES

Ray Charles' first significant public performance occurred when he was a child attending the *Florida School for the Deaf and the Blind.* At age seven, Ray performed *"Jingle Bells"* at a Christmas recital, playing the piano and singing in front of an audience for the first time. Despite his blindness, Ray's musical talent was evident, and this early performance marked the beginning of his journey as a musician. This early public performance had a profound impact on **Ray Charles'** career, showcasing his musical abilities and giving him the confidence to pursue music despite his visual impairment. This experience helped Ray develop resilience and a strong stage presence, later contributing to his success as a pioneering figure in soul music and a renowned performer known for his dynamic live shows.

Ray Charles
Credit – Wikimedia Commons

"I never wanted to be famous. I only wanted to be great."
– Ray Charles

SECTION ONE
PREPARING TO PERFORM

Relax. Breathe. That's all you need to know! But, in case that doesn't seem like enough, here are some great tips:

"Great work is done by people who are not afraid to be great."
— Fernando Flores

OVERCOMING STAGE FRIGHT

My mother always told me to remember when I'm afraid of facing someone, "EVERYONE PUTS THEIR PANTS ON ONE LEG AT A TIME." My most significant tool to overcome stage fright has always been preparation, the knowledge that I'm ready for the task ahead. Here are some other great tips:

BREATHING EXERCISES

Controlled breathing calms the nervous system and reduces anxiety. Inhale deeply into your nose. Hold your breath for a few seconds. Exhale slowly through the mouth. Repeat several times.

4-7-8 Breathing: Inhale for four counts, hold for seven counts, and exhale for eight counts. Repeat this cycle a few times before the performance.

VISUALIZATION TECHNIQUES

Visualize yourself playing the entire piece flawlessly, focusing on the details of your movements and the sound of the music. Picture the audience's positive reaction and imagine feeling calm and confident on stage.

PRACTICE TIPS

Practice performing in front of friends, family, or even a mirror to simulate the performance environment. Break the piece into smaller sections and practice each part thoroughly to build confidence in your ability to play the entire piece. Practice slowly to ensure accuracy and control, gradually increasing the tempo as you become more comfortable. Recording your sessions allows you to listen back from an audience perspective and critique your performances.

SUPPORT NETWORKS

Share your concerns with fellow musicians who understand the challenges of performing and can offer encouragement. Seek guidance from a teacher or mentor who can provide personalized advice and support. Lean on your family and friends for moral support and encouragement. Ask them for constructive feedback.

My friend **Khloe Kardashian** said it best:

"We all have to start somewhere, and doing something is better than nothing at all. Start small so you don't get discouraged and give up. Remember it is all about consistency."

Tad Sisler with Khloe Kardashian and Robin Dougan
Source – Sisler Private Collection

PERFORMANCE PSYCHOLOGY

Practice mindfulness techniques to stay present and focused during the performance, reducing anxiety about potential mistakes. Eliminate negative thoughts. Replace negativity with positive affirmations, like "I am well-prepared" and "I can do this." Accept that some level of anxiety is normal. Anxiety can enhance your performance by keeping you alert and focused.

IMPROVEMENT STRATEGIES

Focus your practice on challenging sections, practice slowly to ensure accuracy, use your metronome, break pieces into manageable segments, and record performances for self-evaluation.

ENGAGING WITH THE AUDIENCE

I'm not an "in your face" performer. I usually let my music do the talking, but I find ways to interact with my audience that are not "over the top." I don't want to criticize other musicians' styles; it's hard enough sometimes to engage an audience, but it bothers me when you go to watch a performance, and a performer is obnoxiously trying too hard to whip the audience into a frenzy. Don't get me wrong. I once went to see **Christopher Cross** in concert. The music was terrific, but he had zero stage presence, and if I didn't love the music so much, I may have been bored stiff. Find a happy medium. Be personable, confident, and kind, and you will be ahead of others. Introduce yourself and the pieces you will play, providing brief, engaging insights about the music. Use facial expressions and body language to convey the emotions of your playing pieces. Make occasional eye contact with the audience to create a sense of connection. Allow natural body movements that reflect the music, such as swaying or expressive hand gestures, without overdoing it.

STAGE PRESENCE

Maintain good posture, standing or sitting upright with relaxed shoulders. Enter and exit the stage with confidence and a smile, acknowledging the audience with a nod or brief eye contact.

BUILDING CONFIDENCE

Thoroughly prepare your pieces to reduce anxiety and increase confidence. Visualize a successful performance and a positive audience response.

AUDIENCE FEEDBACK

Engage with the audience after the performance, thanking them and being open to comments and questions. Listen to positive and constructive feedback and use it to refine and improve your performance.

SOLO VERSUS BAND PERFORMANCE – As a pianist/keyboardist, I approach my solo gigs entirely differently in my technique than when performing with my band. My solo performances have ranged from solo piano to piano and vocals, to piano, drum computer, keyboard bass, and vocals, to keyboards, playing to tracks, and vocals. I know how to play every song, regardless of whether I play along to a track. I also 'overplay' a bit when I'm doing a solo, because I'm covering every base. I play more sparsely with a band to allow other musicians to fill in the holes without creating a cacophony.

SECTION TWO
RECORDING TECHNIQUES

A photograph has been called "a mirror with a memory." In this sense, a recording is a timeless moment that lingers on.

"Songs really are like a form of time travel because they really have moved forward in a bubble. Everyone who's connected with it, the studio's gone, the musicians are gone, and the only thing that's left is this recording which was only about a three-minute period maybe 70 years ago." – Tom Waits

Tom Waits
Credit – Creativecommons.org

HOME RECORDING SETUP

It's hard to predict how technology will look even a few years later. AI has changed the face of progress, and now all the knowledge of the universe is growing exponentially. Still, I believe that the fundamentals of proper recording techniques will remain. Setting up a home recording studio involves essential equipment like acoustic treatment to improve sound quality, a digital audio workstation (DAW) for recording and editing, proper microphone placement to capture the best sound, and recording software for processing and enhancing audio. By understanding and integrating these components, musicians and producers can create high-quality recordings in a home environment.

RECORDING SOFTWARE
AND DIGITAL AUDIO WORKSTATIONS

Recording software captures, edits, and processes audio recordings. DAWs are software platforms for recording, editing, mixing, and producing audio.

Multitrack Recording: Allows recording multiple tracks simultaneously.

Editing Tools: Includes features for cutting, fading, and arranging audio clips.

Effects and Plugins: Offers various effects like reverb, delay, EQ, and compression to enhance recordings.

POPULAR RECORDING SOFTWARE

GarageBand: A free DAW for Mac users with basic recording and editing features, ideal for beginners.

Reaper: Affordable DAW with a wide range of professional features, suitable for all skill levels.

Cubase: Comprehensive DAW with advanced recording, editing, and mixing features.

POPULAR DAWs

Ableton Live: Known for its intuitive interface and robust live performance capabilities.

Logic Pro X: Favored by Mac users for its comprehensive suite of instruments and effects.

Pro Tools: Industry-standard DAW is widely used in professional studios for its powerful editing and mixing features.

FL Studio: Popular among electronic music producers for its user-friendly interface and powerful sequencing capabilities.

I've been a Pro Tools producer and editor for a quarter century. Still, I've also worked on other great platforms like **MOTU's Digital Performer** and **Logic**. It's like learning different languages, where different words and concepts are used to create the same results.

ACOUSTIC TREATMENT

Acoustic treatment involves using materials to control sound reflections, absorption, and diffusion within a recording space to improve sound quality.

Bass Traps: Placed in corners to absorb low frequencies and reduce bass build-up.

Acoustic Panels: Mounted on walls to absorb mid to high frequencies, reducing echo and reverb.

Diffusers: Scatter sound waves to avoid flutter echoes and create a balanced sound environment.

MICROPHONE PLACEMENT

Proper microphone placement is critical to capture the best sound quality. The better-quality microphone, the better the sound. Manufacturers make myriad microphones for different applications, so use a proper microphone for the instrument or vocalist you are recording.

VOCAL RECORDING

Position the microphone at mouth level, 6-12 inches away, and use a pop filter to reduce plosives.

INSTRUMENT RECORDING

Piano: See below

Acoustic Guitar: For a stereo effect, I use two identical high-quality mics; one near the 12th fret, about 6-12 inches away, and the other near the body.

Drum Kit: Use multiple microphones (e.g., overheads, kick, snare) to capture the different elements of the drum set.

Nowadays, great plugins enhance the sound quality of microphones. However, I still run my microphones through my outboard **Avalon** Tube Preamplifiers for a superior sound.

RECORDING YOUR PIANO

The first piano I ever recorded on was an upright, out of tune piano. The detuned sound permeated the session and because of it, the recording sounded amateur. So, first, start with a tuned piano (unless you're doing a ragtime session!). Later, I was blessed during my ten-year gig as a developer for **Yamaha**. We were working on the high-end Disklavier grand pianos, and **Yamaha** issued me a lovely **C3** grand piano that records like a dream. Eventually, I had to purchase the piano at a discount from **Yamaha** to keep it, but it was well worth it, and I've released hundreds of recordings using it. Recording a piano involves setting appropriate levels, choosing the right microphones, and employing effective recording techniques to capture the instrument's full range and character. Careful editing and mixing enhance the recording's clarity and depth, while mastering ensures the final product is polished and consistent.

SETTING LEVELS

Set your input gain so that the loudest parts of the performance peak just below 0 dB (ideally around -6 dB to -3 dB) to avoid clipping. Continuously monitor levels during the recording to ensure consistency.

CHOOSING MICROPHONES

Condensers: Large-diaphragm condensers (e.g., Neumann U87) for a warm, detailed sound.

Small diaphragm condensers (e.g., AKG C414) for a clear, accurate capture.

Pairs: Use matched pairs for stereo recording to achieve a natural and expansive soundstage.

MICROPHONE PLACEMENT / RECORDING

Close Miking: Place one mic above the bass strings and another above the treble strings, a few inches from the strings inside an open grand piano lid, to capture a direct and detailed sound.

Spaced Pair: For a broad stereo image, position two microphones equidistant from the strings, about 3-5 feet apart.

XY Technique: Position two small diaphragm condensers in an XY pattern above the strings for a focused stereo image with good phase coherence.

Room Miking: Place a pair of mics a few feet away from the piano to capture the natural room ambiance, blending with close mics for a fuller sound.

Recording: Ensure a quiet room with good acoustics. Use acoustic treatment to control reflections and resonance. Use closed-back headphones to monitor the sound while recording to ensure clarity and avoid bleed.

EDITING AND MIXING

Editing: Combine the best parts of multiple takes to create a flawless performance. Remove any unwanted noise or mistakes using precise cuts and fades. Adjust timing inconsistencies with tools like quantization if needed but maintain a natural feel.

Mixing: Apply gentle EQ to enhance clarity and balance. Roll off low-end rumble below 50 Hz, boost presence around 5 kHz, and add airiness above 10 kHz if needed. Use light compression to even out dynamics, setting a ratio around 2:1 to 4:1 with a gentle threshold. Add reverb to simulate the piano in a larger space. Use a high-quality reverb plugin to add depth and ambiance without muddying the sound. Pan the close mics slightly left and right to enhance the stereo field.

MASTERING TIPS

When I completed my first "album" in the late 1980s, my record label paid excessive money to **Bernie Grundman's** Mastering House in Los Angeles, California, one of the very best in the nation at that time, for mastering. Now, you can do it all using excellent plugins with a good ear. Mastering ensures the final recording is polished, balanced, and ready for distribution. Make subtle EQ adjustments to ensure the recording sounds balanced on different playback systems. Apply a limiter to prevent clipping and slightly increase the overall loudness without losing dynamics. Compare the mastered track with reference recordings to ensure competitive loudness and tonal balance. Export the final master in current high-quality formats like WAV for distribution and MP3 for online sharing.

PRODUCING HIGH-QUALITY RECORDINGS

I could spend much time on the nuances of using your DAW software to record a mix most efficiently. Producing high-quality recordings involves layering tracks for depth, adding effects to enhance sound, using virtual instruments for versatility, balancing the mix for clarity, and finalizing the track through mastering. Producers can create professional-sounding recordings that stand out by following the following steps. Make sure that you always use the highest bit rates available for recording.

LAYERING TRACKS

Layering involves recording multiple tracks to create a rich, full sound. Record multiple takes of the same instrument and layer them to add depth. Using different instruments or sounds to layer similar parts creates a more complex texture. Pan tracks left and right to spread the sound across the stereo field, enhancing spatial dimension.

ADDING EFFECTS

Add reverb to simulate natural space and add depth. Use delay to create echo effects and add rhythmic complexity. Apply EQ to adjust the frequency balance, removing unwanted frequencies and enhancing desired ones. Use compression to control dynamics, ensuring consistent levels and adding punch to the sound.

USING VIRTUAL INSTRUMENTS

Virtual instruments (VSTs) are software-based instruments that emulate real instruments and synth sounds. I've had the best success using an actual instrument for the primary recording, like a trumpet and saxophone for a horn section or a violin and cello for strings, and then layering virtual instruments underneath the real ones for a more authentic sound. Choose high-quality VSTs that suit the genre and desired sound. Program realistic performances using MIDI, paying attention to velocity, articulation, and expression. Combine multiple virtual instruments to create richer textures and more dynamic arrangements.

BALANCING THE MIX

Adjust the volume of each track to ensure that all elements are heard clearly without overpowering each other. Spread instruments across the stereo field to create a balanced and spacious mix. Use EQ to carve out space for each instrument, avoiding frequency clashes and ensuring clarity.

FINALIZING THE TRACK involves mastering, which prepares the mix for distribution by optimizing its overall sound. Make subtle EQ adjustments to ensure the track sounds balanced on different playback systems. Apply a limiter to prevent clipping and increase loudness without sacrificing dynamics. Ensure the track has a consistent volume and tonal balance compared to other professional tracks. Export the final master in high-quality formats like WAV for distribution and MP3 for online sharing.

SECTION THREE
SHARING YOUR MUSIC

We live in an era like none before. You no longer need a huge record label to become a viral success. With a good product and persistence, you can go all the way. Building an online presence as a pianist or musician involves leveraging social media platforms, creating a professional website, engaging consistently with fans, producing diverse content, implementing effective marketing strategies, and utilizing AI tools. By integrating these elements, you can expand your reach, grow your fanbase, and enhance career opportunities.

"I believe musicians have a duty, a responsibility to reach out, to share your love or pain with others." — James Taylor

James Taylor
Credit – Wikimedia Commons via Picryl.com

SOCIAL MEDIA PLATFORMS: As this book is published, these are the most valuable platforms for sharing:

Instagram: Share photos, short videos, and stories to give a behind-the-scenes look at your musical journey.

Facebook: Create a musician page to share updates and events and connect with a broad audience.

YouTube: Upload performance videos, tutorials, and vlogs to showcase your talent and personality.

X: Share quick updates, interact with fans, and join conversations about music.

TikTok: Post short, engaging clips of performances, practice sessions, and creative content to reach a younger audience.

Truth Social: Post anything patriotic or Americana to reach this expanding audience.

CREATING A WEBSITE: Today, a personal website is a central hub for all information about your music career. Tomorrow, new advancements in technology will offer different platforms, but we assume the content will be close to the same:

Homepage: Include a professional photo, a brief bio, and links to your social media profiles.

Music: Embed your music from platforms like Spotify, Apple Music, or SoundCloud.

Events: List upcoming performances, tours, and events.

Blog: Share updates, insights, and articles about your music and experiences.

Contact: Provide a contact form or email address for booking inquiries and fan communication.

ENGAGING WITH FANS: Building a loyal fanbase requires consistent engagement and interaction. Reply to comments on social media posts and YouTube videos. Host live Q&A sessions, virtual concerts, and practice sessions to connect with fans in real time. Organize contests and giveaways to encourage fan participation and show appreciation.

CONTENT CREATION: Share videos of live performances, studio sessions, and covers. Create educational content like tutorials, tips, and practice routines. Post behind-the-scenes content to give fans a glimpse into your creative process. Collaborate with other musicians to reach their audiences and create fresh content.

MARKETING STRATEGIES: Collect email addresses and send regular newsletters with updates, exclusive content, and event announcements. Targeted ads on social media platforms and Google can be used to reach potential fans. Optimize your website with SEO content for search engines to increase visibility. Monitor engagement and analytics to understand what resonates with your unique audience. Adjust your strategy accordingly.

USING ARTIFICIAL INTELLIGENCE: Use AI tools to generate social media posts, blog content, and video ideas. Analyse your music with AI tools to understand its strengths and areas for improvement. Use AI to personalize fan interactions and recommend content based on their preferences. Leverage AI-driven marketing tools for targeted advertising and campaign optimization.

DEVELOPING A CAREER PLAN: The first thing we all need to do is prioritize what we want to accomplish in the music business. As a young performer, I wanted to be a pop star with hits on the BILLBOARD TOP 100 chart. I also knew I might have a better chance at that if I performed regularly, so I started to get solo gigs playing piano and singing in bars and nightclubs. I put together a band and began working off-nights at clubs until I got a full-time gig. At some point, I moved over to corporate events, traveling and working many different styles: One night, we would be a jazz trio, and the next, an Awards Banquet big band. The next night, we might do a Beach party, and then another night, we were a Motown Revue. I had my core players, and I would hire others to match the genre, and I did very well over a long period.

MAKING MONEY WITH MUSIC: As of May 2023, there were approximately 35,520 employed musicians and singers in the **United States**. The median hourly wage for professional musicians was $39.14. The lowest 10% earned less than $16.02 per hour, while the highest 10% earned more than $102.98 per hour. -source, Bureau of Labor Statistics

It's disconcerting to find that many musicians will work for almost nothing just for the opportunity to perform. My dear friend **Shari Kelley**, an extraordinary event planner, once told me I wasn't charging enough for my performances. She suggested that if I raised my price, clients would believe they were getting a better-quality band, and she was right. I earned more respect as I earned more money. As a bandleader, you can earn more by scheduling events, providing and setting up all equipment, coordinating musicians, and dealing with event planners. However, don't underpay your musicians, or you will find it hard to find good musicians to work with regularly. To provide for my family appropriately, I worked multiple gigs at once. I performed poolside at hotels during the day, did corporate gigs at night, and worked in nightclubs on off-nights for years. Eventually, to stay in the music business, I put together my recording studio, learned how to produce and edit, and branched out again to promote concerts and book other artists. You can do whatever it takes if you want it bad enough.

I can give you a hundred ways to advance your career, but, as my friend, former Secretary of State, **General Colin Powell,** said:

"There are no secrets to success. It is the result of preparation, hard work, and learning from failure."

Tad Sisler with Secretary of State, General Colin Powell
Source: Tad Sisler's personal collection

Choose the journey you want to take, and if you're not sure, here are some strategies and avenues you can explore:

LIVE PERFORMANCES – One of the most traditional ways to make money playing piano/keyboards is through live performances and gigs at local venues like bars, clubs, restaurants, or coffee houses. Many couples hire pianists to perform at their weddings for ceremonies, receptions, or first dances. Corporate events, private parties, and fundraisers often require live entertainment, providing many opportunities to showcase your talent and earn income. I've done all these and worked full-time performing, making enough income to raise four kids and live comfortably during that period. But I worked my tail off, moving equipment, performing long hours, sometimes 2 or 3 gigs a day, to do it.

LIVE PERFORMANCE HACK: I've performed for over a decade at the same nightclub three different times in my career. My secret is that I make sure I have a diverse repertoire, and I change my vocal and piano performance style to match each genre, so every song does not sound the same. This diversity in my repertoire not only keeps my audience engaged but also gives me a sense of pride in my versatility. Have you ever seen a performer and liked them, but it's like everything sounds the same after a while? Avoid being boring at all costs. Also, don't be surprised that no matter how many songs you learn, people will want to hear the same fifty most popular songs every night if you're willing to play them, songs like "Piano Man," "Brown Eyed Girl," "Mustang Sally," etc. It's a test of your commitment and perseverance to keep delivering what your audience wants, even if it means playing the same songs repeatedly.

SESSION KEYBOARDIST – Most of the performing and touring musicians I know do many sessions between their live performances. Some have become just session musicians who make a good living as first-call performers. Session playing involves recording parts for other artists, producers, and composers, including piano, keyboards, synths, lead parts, and solos for commercial recordings, jingles, film soundtracks, and television commercials. Session players often work in recording studios and are compensated for their talent and time. You can make yourself more valuable if you double on an instrument, and even more so if you can set up a professional home studio, import tracks and play them in your own environment, provide quality performance, and send the session back, saving the producer time. Most producers will want to direct your performance themselves. Still, when you become more studied, many producers will do anything to save time and keep the ball rolling.

SESSION SONGWRITER – If you have songwriting or jingle writing skills besides singing, you can collaborate with other songwriters, musicians, and producers to write and record original songs for commercial release. This collaborative aspect of session work not only enhances the quality of the music but also makes you feel part of a vibrant music community. Session work can also involve pitching songs to recording artists, music publishers, and music licensing agencies for placement in films, television shows, and advertisements. You can register as a songwriter and publisher with a **Performing Rights Organization** like **BMI, ASCAP, SOCAN,** or whatever organization is based in your country.

TEACHER/VOCAL COACH – If you have music theory and harmony expertise, you can offer private piano lessons and coaching sessions to aspiring pianists of all skill levels. My granddaughter **Makayla Phillips**, drawing on her experience competing on *America's Got Talent* and *American Idol,* has set up a fairly lucrative little business doing online coaching for singers all over when she's not busy performing or recording. Teaching can provide a steady income stream, allowing you to share your knowledge and passion for performing with others.

BANDS AND ENSEMBLES – Working with other skilled musicians propels you in many ways, from advancing your technique to social interaction. Many bands and ensembles provide opportunities for paid performances, competitions, and recording projects.

STREET PERFORMANCE involves performing in public spaces like parks, streets, and subway stations. While income can be unpredictable, it can provide exposure and tips from people passing by. Some cities require street-performing permits, so be sure to check local regulations. A municipality or street fair often paid my band to perform at larger, coordinated outside events. **Joni Mitchell** wrote a great song about this, called *Real Good For Free,* which was also covered by **David Crosby** shortly before his passing.

CRUISE SHIPS – Many cruise lines employ piano players, small ensembles, and show bands as entertainment staff to perform in their onboard theatres, cabarets, and lounges. Cruise ship performers typically receive room, board, and a salary, and it's a great way to see the world. Years ago, **Jesse Lopez** (a great cruise ship singer and the brother of my friend, legendary artist **Trini Lopez**) sat me down and told me that if you're going to go on a cruise as a singer, to make sure that you are billed as a headliner. He said headliners are given better accommodations and dine with the guests. At the same time, regular musicians and bands work very hard and are placed below the hold with the other staff on a cruise ship. Nevertheless, it is a great way to travel and make money. When I was a boy, many older men I met would tell me they joined the **Merchant Marines** to see the world when they were young. Unfortunately, my father's generation had to fight in World War II to see the world, and many never returned. Cruises are great, especially if you do not have kids yet, because being away from family for long periods can be challenging for many of us.

MUSICAL THEATRE – If you have acting skills and singing talent, consider auditioning for roles in musical theatre productions. The musical theatre industry offers a promising avenue for growth, with opportunities to earn salaries or stipends for your work in touring shows, stage productions, and regional theatre companies. Who knows, you could end up on Broadway! My friend, extraordinary drummer **Andrew Fraga, Jr.,** toured with orchestras in tours of **Broadway** musicals as a percussionist, including *"Oklahoma"* and *"Fiddler on the Roof."* He enjoyed it immensely; it broadened him as a performer, and he was compensated well enough to make it worthwhile. I was hired and paid many times as a rehearsal pianist for big shows including the **Palm Springs Follies**, and the **National Dance Institute,** led by the famous dancer **Jacque d'Amboise.**

ONLINE – We've already touched on the value of social media. The online world is a powerful tool for musicians, allowing you to showcase your unique performance talent and reach a wider audience. In today's world, online platforms are essential. **YouTube, Instagram, TikTok**, and **Facebook** are not just for sharing videos of performances, original songs, and covers, but also for monetizing your content through sponsorships, advertising, merchandise sales, and fan donations. Many friends utilized this during the COVID-19 shutdown in the early 2020s. They could keep performing from home while somewhat compensated through donations from their friends.

STREAMING—Although streaming royalties may not initially provide substantial income, building a loyal fan base and effectively promoting your music on **Spotify, Apple Music, Amazon Music, Pandora**, and other platforms can increase your streaming revenue over time. You can also sell digital downloads and merchandise through online music stores and platforms such as **Bandcamp** and **CD Baby**. I have hundreds of tracks up on **CD Baby** on all platforms, and I make a little money each month from streams and sales.

FAN SUPPORT – Engage with your supporters and fans through crowdfunding platforms like **Kickstarter, GoFundMe,** and **Patreon**. Offer exclusive content, experiences, and rewards in exchange for monthly subscriptions or one-time donations. This direct-to-fan approach can provide sustainable income and strengthen your audience's connection. My friend and legendary big-band saxophonist **Ron Aprea** recently crowdfunded an excellent album of swing music fronted by his lovely wife, **Angela DeNiro**. If you're into that kind of music, you will love the arrangements and vocals.

LICENSING – This remains probably the most substantial vehicle for good moneymaking in music. However, it may be tough to break into initially. Explore opportunities to license your music in films, video games, commercials, television shows, and other media projects. Music supervisors, production companies, and licensing agencies often seek original songs and covers for synchronization with visual content. Register your music with a **P.R.O.** like **ASCAP, BMI, SESAC,** etc., to collect royalties from public performances and broadcasts. Over the years, I've had a ton of music placed in television shows, feature films, and ads. A production company has often called on me to create a soundalike track or a song with a particular vibe to match their project.

MERCHANDISING – Many friends in touring bands develop merchandise like T-shirts, hats, posters, and other branded merchandise to sell at live performances and online. Collaborate with brands and sponsors for endorsement deals, product placements, and sponsored content opportunities. Being aligned with compatible brands can provide additional income, validation, and exposure for your music career. I have friends from my *Yamaha* days, great performers who *Yamaha* endorsed. It's a great endorsement and comes with free instruments and other perks.

FESTIVALS/COMPETITIONS – You can apply to perform at music festivals, talent competitions, state fairs, and on the college circuit, which has proven to be a great source of income and exposure for many of my friends. Winning or placing in competitions can lead to prize money, performance opportunities, and industry recognition. Additionally, participating in industry events and music conferences can help you connect with industry professionals and advance your career. **Makayla Phillips** entered regional singing competitions as a young teenager. At the age of 14, she won the regional competition *Temecula Idol,* which put her on the radar to audition for *America's Got Talent* , leading to her **Golden Buzzer** moment with **Heidi Klum** at just 15 years old.

COLLABORATIONS – Engaging in collaborations with producers, DJs, or fellow artists can significantly benefit your music career. By featuring as a guest vocalist on tracks or working on remixes and original songs, you can broaden your fan base and open up new income opportunities.

PUBLISHING – If you are an original songwriter, consider signing with a music publisher or establishing your own music publishing company to administer your rights to your music. Music publishers can help secure placements for your songs with major star artists, films, television shows, commercials, and other media projects, as well as collect royalties from mechanical licenses, performance rights, and sync deals. Many friends have moved to **Nashville** to pursue this avenue; some have hooked up with influential labels and publishers.

CORPORATE EVENTS – Performing at corporate events, private parties, weddings, and special occasions as a soloist or with a band can be a lucrative way to make money on a full-time basis. Agencies, companies, and individuals hire musicians to provide live entertainment for their events, offering opportunities for paid performances and networking with potential collaborators and clients. When I started out doing this, I hooked up with an agent who controlled the corporate entertainment of several of the large hotels and convention centres in my area. Because of the number of conventions and private events agents booked for me regularly, I could quit my regular gig and work full-time doing corporate and private parties. It was a lot of setting up and breaking down my equipment, but every night was a different vibe, and I also worked many day events. The financial security and variety of opportunities are advantageous.

HOW TO HANDLE CORPORATE EVENTS: Create a checklist of all equipment, instruments, wires, stands, microphones, speakers, computers, and anything else you need for the gig. You don't want to show up without an essential instrument or stand. Eventually, you'll only need a mental checklist. After breaking down our equipment at the end of each gig, we do what we call the "idiot check," going back and checking around and under the stage for anything we might have missed. Early arrival at events is crucial. It not only provides you with sufficient time to set up your equipment and address any unforeseen issues but also reassures the event planner. Remember, people tend to arrive early, so be ready to perform at least 15 minutes before your scheduled start time.

Watch your volume, especially during cocktail hours and dinner sets when people like to talk. Always look your best. Grooming and proper dress are essential for corporate gigs. Be accommodating and classy. Attitudes and emotions power everything you do. Do not eat food or drink alcohol unless the client specifically approves it. Always choose appropriate music for the moment.

Don't take long breaks unless it fits within the client's schedule. I was working a nightclub gig with a trio in **Palm Springs,** and it was a prolonged night, so we took an exceptionally long break. My saxophonist Pat **Rizzo** looked at me and said, *"We'd better go back and play. It's almost time for our next break!"* I loved that joke, but I promise clients and bar owners always look at the time and expect you to take regular breaks. Most musicians play sets of 45 minutes to an hour. The usual break time is fifteen minutes. I've done nights where the client asked in advance for continuous music without breaks, and that's what they get from me. I charged accordingly.

TALENT SHOWS—Like music festivals and competitions, talent shows allow you to gain exposure while you showcase your talent. Winning or placing in these competitions can lead to prize money, recording contracts, and other opportunities to advance your music career. Participating in talent showcases can also help you build confidence and connect with industry professionals and fellow musicians.

NEPOTISM – It shouldn't surprise you that a large part of gaining success in this competitive profession is knowing someone on the inside. A friend or family member in a powerful position at a film company, television network, agency, publisher, advertising agency, or management company can open doors for you in a heartbeat. It's a fact of life in this business. If you know someone golden, you are golden. This reality, while challenging, also offers a glimmer of hope and possibility for aspiring musicians.

My friend, actor **Lorenzo Lamas**, said:

"You go and find work wherever it is, and you learn from it. No matter what the experience is, you can always file something away as knowledge."

Tad Sisler with Lorenzo Lamas and A.J. Lamas
Source: Tad Sisler's Personal Collection

The only true 'secret' to becoming a great pianist or keyboardist is practice and endless repetition until you've mastered your craft.

CHAPTER SEVEN
DEVELOPING A PERSONAL PRACTICE ROUTINE

Regular practice as a musician significantly enhances skill development, with studies showing that consistent, deliberate practice can lead to a 25% improvement in performance accuracy and technique over time. Research from the **Journal of Research in Music Education** indicates that musicians who practice daily demonstrate faster cognitive processing speeds and better memory retention compared to non-musicians.

The **Royal Conservatory of Music** also found that students who engage in regular, focused practice sessions are 60% more likely to achieve higher grades in music exams, highlighting the profound impact of disciplined practice on musical proficiency and overall skill advancement.

SECTION ONE
STRUCTURING PRACTICE
SETTING GOALS AND SCHEDULES

A well-structured practice routine for a pianist involves setting clear goals, tracking progress, adjusting goals as needed, creating a consistent practice schedule, balancing technical exercises with repertoire, incorporating rest periods, and finding ways to stay motivated.

Short-Term Goals: Focus on specific techniques or pieces, such as mastering a problematic passage or improving sight-reading.

Long-Term Goals: Aim for broader achievements like preparing for a recital or completing a graded exam.

TRACKING PROGRESS

Keep a daily journal noting what you practiced, challenges faced, and improvements made. Make audio or video recordings to track progress over time.

ADJUSTING GOALS

Weekly or monthly review sessions to adjust goals and set new targets. Be willing to adjust your goals based on progress and unexpected challenges.

CREATING A PRACTICE SCHEDULE

Choose specific times each day for practice, focusing on different aspects like warm-ups, technique, and repertoire. Plan broader goals for the week, such as mastering certain sections of a piece or improving specific skills.

BALANCING TECHNIQUES AND REPERTOIRE

Spend time on scales, arpeggios, and finger exercises to build a solid technical foundation. Work on pieces of varying styles and difficulties to develop musicality and performance skills.

INCORPORATING REST

Take short breaks during practice sessions to rest your hands and mind. Schedule regular rest days to allow for recovery and reflection.

STAYING MOTIVATED

Include fun pieces and challenging exercises to keep practice interesting. Reward yourself for reaching milestones and completing goals. Engage with fellow musicians, teachers, or online communities for support and inspiration.

As we've mentioned already, use focused practice, slow everything down while practicing perfecting the section or piece, use a metronome, chunk difficult sections, and stay mindful throughout. It's not always fun. It can be tedious, but remember what legendary pianist **Tori Amos** said:

"Sometimes you have to do what you don't like to get to where you want to be."

Tori Amos

SECTION TWO
OVERCOMING PRACTICE CHALLENGES

We've discussed dealing with frustration, breaking down challenges, keeping a positive mindset, seeking help from others when needed, celebrating small victories, and staying patient. We've also touched on avoiding burnout, varying your practice routines, taking breaks, using relaxation techniques, and finding inspiration by enjoying the process. Remember to stay consistent, build habits, and be accountable to yourself. If you can find a practice partner or join a community for regular assessment, you will easily overcome any challenges and shine!

"It's part of life to have obstacles. It's about overcoming obstacles; that's the key to happiness." – Herbie Hancock

ENHANCING PRACTICE WITH TECHNOLOGY

Musicians can optimize their practice sessions, track their progress, and continually improve their skills by incorporating metronome and tuner apps, sheet music management tools, online tutorials, interactive practice platforms, and recording software.

USEFUL APPS AND TOOLS

Metronome Apps: Digital metronomes like **Pro Metronome** and **Metronome Beats** provide precise tempo control with customizable features, helping musicians maintain consistent rhythm and timing during practice.

Tuner Apps: Apps like **TonalEnergy Tuner** and **Cleartune** offer accurate instrument tuning, ensuring that musicians are always in tune.

Sheet Music Apps: **forScore** and **MuseScore** allow musicians to store, organize, and annotate digital sheet music, making it easier to access and manage their repertoire.

ONLINE RESOURCES

Video Tutorials and Masterclasses: Platforms like **YouTube** and **MasterClass** provide access to instructional videos and masterclasses from renowned musicians, offering insights and techniques to enhance playing skills.

Practice Tools: Websites like **SmartMusic** and **MusicNotes** offer interactive practice tools, play-along tracks, and extensive music libraries to support musicians' practice routines.

Online Courses: **Coursera** and **Udemy** offer comprehensive music courses covering theory, technique, and performance, allowing musicians to learn at their own pace.

INCORPORATING TECH INTO PRACTICE

Recording Software: Digital Audio Workstations (DAWs) like **GarageBand** and **Audacity** allow musicians to record and analyze their practice sessions, helping identify areas for improvement and track progress over time.

Backing Tracks and Accompaniment: Apps like **iReal Pro** provide customizable backing tracks for various genres, enabling musicians to practice improvisation and performance with a virtual band.

Interactive Learning: Tools like **Yousician** and **Simply Piano** offer interactive lessons and real-time feedback, making practice sessions engaging and effective (see our section on AI-powered apps for more suggestions).

Virtual Collaboration: Platforms like **Soundtrap** and **BandLab** enable musicians to collaborate remotely, recording and sharing their parts with bandmates or instructors.

Everything starts and ends in our minds and hearts. Learning an instrument offers many psychological and emotional benefits, above and beyond learning techniques. Trying and failing, and then trying again are crucial elements of becoming not only a strong performer but a strong person. My dear old friend, legendary actress **Mary Tyler Moore** said it best:

"You can't be brave if you've only had wonderful things happen to you."

Tad Sisler and Mary Tyler Moore
Source- Sisler Private Collection

CHAPTER EIGHT
PSYCHOLOGICAL ASPECTS
OF LEARNING AN INSTRUMENT

SECTION ONE
BUILDING CONFIDENCE
OVERCOMING SELF DOUBT

You can often mitigate self-doubt through positive self-talk and visualization techniques. Positive self-talk involves consciously replacing negative thoughts with affirmations and constructive statements. For example, instead of thinking, "I'll never master this piece," tell yourself, "I am improving with every practice session." This shift in mindset can significantly boost confidence and motivation.

Visualization techniques can build self-assurance and reduce anxiety by allowing you to mentally rehearse performances and picture successful outcomes.

My early days of praying for guidance and confidence before I went into my first gigs were all about visualizing my success. Fear is an impostor. My dear friend **Frank Hamblen**, 7-time Championship-Winning *NBA* Coach, used to say:

"You just refuse to lose. True success is found in the relentless pursuit of excellence and the unwavering belief in your own potential."

Frank Hamblen and Tad Sisler
Source: Tad Sisler's Personal Collection

SETTING ACHIEVABLE GOALS

By breaking down larger, long-term goals into smaller, manageable tasks, musicians can make the process less daunting and celebrate more frequent successes. For instance, instead of aiming to perfect an entire piece in one go, a musician might focus on mastering a few measures each day. Celebrating these small victories is equally important.

BUILDING A SUPPORT NETWORK

Finally, seeking support from teachers, mentors, peers, and loved ones offers camaraderie and mutual encouragement.

DEVELOPING A GROWTH MINDSET

Musicians should view complex pieces or techniques as valuable learning experiences that can enhance their skills. Instead of shying away from complex tasks, they should approach them with curiosity and determination.

PERSISTENCE AND RESILIENCE

The path to musical mastery is often long and filled with setbacks, but maintaining a persistent attitude helps musicians overcome these hurdles. Even when progress seems slow, practicing regularly builds resilience and fosters a deeper understanding of the instrument.

"Nothing in this world can take the place of persistence. Talent will not; nothing is more common than unsuccessful men with talent. Genius will not; unrewarded genius is almost a proverb. Education will not; the world is full of educated derelicts. Persistence and determination alone are omnipotent. The slogan 'Press On!' has solved and always will solve the problems of the human race." — *Calvin Coolidge*

STAYING CURIOUS

Always be open to exploring different genres, techniques, and theories. This curiosity drives innovation and keeps the learning process exciting and dynamic. Seeking encouragement and guidance from mentors can significantly support your journey to help you navigate challenges more effectively.

ACHIEVING MILESTONES

Break milestones into smaller, manageable tasks that you can accomplish progressively. For example, instead of aiming to master an entire concerto, a pianist might set a milestone to learn the first movement within a month. Recognize and celebrate these achievements.

REFLECTING AND PLANNING

Regularly reviewing your accomplishments helps you understand your growth trajectory and identify areas for further improvement.

Even those of us who have achieved great milestones have the human tendency to become discouraged. My friend, legendary actress **Dyan Cannon**, said:

"I have become down-hearted. I have become discouraged. I have become depressed. I'm just like you. I'm a human being and I have my problems."

It all comes down to attitudes and emotions. Overcoming fear and getting beyond discouragement or disappointment is all part of the human condition and one of the marvellous ways we can get there is by feeling the joy of accomplishment and creating something new. Press on, always, and believe that things can get better. Every day we have a new opportunity to reinvent ourselves.

Dyan Cannon and Tad Sisler
Source- Sisler Private Collection

While you're learning this magical instrument, you will encounter frustration, even exasperation as you attempt to improve. Endless repetition and maintaining your passion for performing will carry you through even the darkest times.

Remember the words of **Dr. Norman Vincent Peale**:

"There is only one group of people who do not have problems, and they are all dead. Problems are a sign of life, so the more problems you have, the more alive you are."

SECTION TWO
COGNITIVE BENEFITS OF LEARNING MUSIC

My father, **Maynard Lee Sisler**, was a physician specializing in internal medicine. He learned medicine on the spot as a medic on a Navy ship in World War II. Doctors were scarce in the South Pacific, so my father quickly learned to diagnose sailors and do emergency surgery when needed. Years later, after extensive training in medical school, he told me that the most important thing a doctor can do is to listen to their patients. In their own way, they will tell you what you need to know to help them. I believe it's the same with all of us. We must learn to listen to ourselves and what our body and mind tell us. Most of what is wrong with us can be helped immensely by exercise, eating right, and getting enough sleep. Learning to play an instrument is one of the best things you can do for your long-term cognitive ability. In fact, playing piano in particular has been linked to better brain health in older adults, according to a recent study published in *Science Daily*.

Maynard Lee Sisler, M.D., F.A.C.P
Source – Sisler Private collection

ENHANCING MEMORY
Techniques for memorizing music include breaking the piece into smaller sections and practicing each part repetitively until it is internalized. Brain exercises, such as sight-reading and transposing music, also help develop a musician's memory. Repetition and recall are crucial, as repeatedly playing sections of a piece strengthens neural pathways, making it easier to remember.

ASSOCIATION TECHNIQUES, such as linking a passage of music to a specific emotion, story, or visual image, can enhance recall. This method makes the music more meaningful and creates a personal connection to the piece, making it easier to remember.

IMPROVING FOCUS AND CONCENTRATION
Music practice is a discipline that improves focus and concentration. It requires sustained attention, discipline, and focused practice sessions, where specific goals are set and distractions are minimized, to enhance these cognitive skills. Eliminating distractions such as mobile phones and creating a quiet practice environment are not just suggestions but commitments to maintaining concentration.

STRUCTURED ROUTINES
Regular practice at the same time each day helps build discipline and enhances cognitive functions like memory and attention. Incorporating mental exercises, such as practicing a piece in your mind without physically playing the

instrument, can also improve musical memory and understanding. This method, known as mental rehearsal, engages the brain similarly to physical practice and can reinforce learning. The cognitive benefits of learning music, including improved memory, focus, and concentration, contribute to a musician's overall mental understanding and effectiveness in both musical and non-musical tasks.

When it comes to playing the piano, I've always been "all-in." Single-mindedness goes a long way when you put your mind to achieving a task. My old friend, legendary actor **Gene Barry**, spoke of his dream:

> *"My earliest dreams were of acting, and I have never considered anything else."*

Make it your mantra to improve even slightly every day.

Tad, Rachel and Stephanie Sisler with Gene Barry
Source – Sisler Private Collection

BOOSTING CREATIVITY: Composing music allows for exploring original melodies and harmonies, providing a unique outlet for self-expression. Experimenting with different sounds and genres broadens your musical palette and inspires new approaches to playing. Collaborating with other musicians introduces diverse perspectives and ideas, fostering creative synergy. Additionally, setting creative challenges, such as writing a piece in an unfamiliar style or improvising within specific constraints, can push the boundaries of your creativity and lead to innovative musical discoveries.

SECTION THREE
EMOTIONAL AND SOCIAL BENEFITS

My sister, **Suzanne Ramsey**, was a trained psychologist and a mental health center director for many years. She told me that she found in many patients that simple stress and burnout were the cause of many mental health issues. Fears, including fear of failure or disappointment, were other leading issues beyond simple depression based upon loss. Learning to sing or play an instrument can help to alleviate many mental health issues. My sister had many tools to help her patients, and music therapy was among those tools.

Suzanne Ramsey and Tad Sisler
Source- Sisler Private Collection

STRESS RELIEF AND RELAXATION

Engaging in regular piano practice can serve as a powerful form of therapy, providing an outlet for emotions and a means to unwind. The repetitive nature of playing scales, arpeggios, and familiar pieces can be meditative, helping to lower stress levels and promote relaxation. Additionally, employing relaxation techniques such as deep breathing and mindfulness while playing can further enhance the calming effects of piano practice. Music is a profound medium for emotional expression, and pianists often find joy in conveying their innermost thoughts and emotions through their instruments. Whether playing a soothing nocturne or an exhilarating concerto, the emotional range of the piano provides a canvas for expressing a broad spectrum of emotions.

BUILDING SOCIAL CONNECTIONS

A pianist can build social connections by actively joining music groups and ensembles. Participation in local or school bands, choirs, and orchestras provides performance opportunities. It fosters a sense of community among musicians. Engaging in workshops and masterclasses is another excellent way to connect with others with similar interests and goals. Take my advice about using online resources outlined in this book.

PERSONAL FULFILLMENT

Setting personal goals, such as mastering a challenging piece, improving specific techniques, or composing original music, provides a sense of purpose and direction. Achieving these goals, no matter how small, brings a deep sense of accomplishment and progress. Additionally, working towards long-term dreams, such as performing at prestigious venues, recording an album, or earning a music degree, fuels motivation and dedication.

Performing for audiences, whether in intimate settings or grand concert halls, allows pianists to connect with listeners on an emotional level and share their artistic expression. This act of sharing can inspire others, fostering a love for music in students, peers, and audiences alike. Knowing that their music has touched someone's life or motivated another to pursue their musical dreams can be incredibly gratifying. Moreover, embracing the lifelong journey of learning and growing as a musician keeps the passion alive, ensuring that the pursuit of personal fulfillment through music remains an ever-evolving and profoundly enriching experience, inspiring others to embark on their musical journey.

Victor Frankl endured the horrors of a concentration camp during the Holocaust in World War II. In his book, **"Man's Search for Meaning,"** he described that the one thing that couldn't be taken from him was his ability to decide how he would handle any situation, no matter how bad. He also said:

"Everyone has his [or her] own specific vocation or mission in life; everyone must carry out a concrete assignment that demands fulfillment. Therein, he cannot be replaced, nor can his life be repeated; thus, everyone's task is unique as his specific opportunity to implement it."

Victor Frankl
Credit – Wikimedia Commons

CHAPTER NINE
ADVANCED PRACTICE TECHNIQUES AND STRATEGIES

"Prayer is when you talk to God. Meditation is when you're listening. Playing the piano allows you to do both at the same time."
– Kelsey Grammer

SECTION ONE
ADVANCED TECHNICAL EXERCISES

EXTENDED SCALES

Extended scales go beyond the basic major and minor scales, incorporating additional notes and different tonalities that give a pianist's repertoire more colour. Go back and perfect the harmonic minor scale, which raises the seventh note of the natural minor scale, creating a leading tone, and the melodic minor scale, raising both the sixth and seventh notes when ascending and reverting to the natural minor when descending.

Practice the whole tone scale, composed entirely of whole steps, and the diminished scale, alternating between whole and half steps.

COMPLEX ARPEGGIOS

Complex arpeggios involve playing the notes of extended chords in a broken fashion, creating flowing, cascading patterns. These include arpeggios of seventh chords (e.g., dominant seventh, major seventh, minor seventh), ninth chords, and altered chords. Playing these arpeggios requires precise finger coordination and fluid motion across the keyboard. For instance, an arpeggio of a C major seventh chord (C, E, G, B) or a C minor ninth chord (C, Eb, G, Bb, D) introduces more complexity. It demands a higher level of technical proficiency.

PRACTICE TECHNIQUE

Using a metronome helps maintain a consistent tempo and ensures evenness in playing. Gradually increasing the speed as comfort with the pattern grows is recommended. Hands-separate practice can initially aid in mastering the fingerings before integrating both hands. Additionally, during practice, varying rhythms and articulations (e.g., staccato, legato) can provide a more thorough understanding and control of the scales and arpeggios.

INCORPORATING INTO MUSIC

Incorporating complex scales and arpeggios into music involves understanding their harmonic and melodic functions within a piece. For instance, harmonic minor and melodic minor scales can add tension and resolve in compositions, especially in classical and jazz contexts. Arpeggios of extended chords can be integrated into improvisations or used to embellish melodic lines.

DAILY EXERCISES

Dedicating a portion of each practice session to these elements ensures steady progress and fluency. Exercises might include playing scales and arpeggios in different keys, using varied rhythms and dynamics, or exploring different inversions and fingerings.

SPEED AND ACCURACY DRILLS

METRONOME EXERCISES: To begin, set the metronome at a slow tempo, allowing for precise execution of each note. Practice scales, arpeggios, and passages of music, ensuring every note aligns perfectly with the metronome clicks. As proficiency improves, incrementally increase the tempo, focusing on maintaining accuracy.

GRADUAL SPEED INCREASES: Start by practicing a passage or exercise at a comfortable tempo where accuracy is maintained. Once confident, increase the tempo slightly and practice until it feels as controlled as the slower speed.

This process should be repeated, increasing the tempo in small increments. This technique, often called "speed bursts," involves playing a few measures at a faster tempo and then returning to a slower pace. This helps the fingers and brain adapt to the increased speed without sacrificing accuracy.

PRECISION TECHNIQUES: Precision techniques focus on clean execution and control. One effective method is to practice hands separately before combining them. This allows each hand to master its part independently, reducing the cognitive load when playing hands together. Another technique is to practice with varying articulations, such as staccato and legato, to ensure control over finger pressure and movement. Additionally, isolating and repeating difficult passages helps to iron out any inaccuracies. Using a mirror to observe hand movements can also provide insights into any unnecessary motions that may hinder precision.

FINGER DEXTERITY EXERCISES

Exercises like **Hanon, Czerny,** and **Dohnányi** focus on developing finger strength and control. Practicing scales and arpeggios with different rhythms and dynamics in various keys enhances finger coordination and speed. Additionally, exercises that involve finger substitutions and crossovers can improve dexterity, muscle memory, and the ability to navigate complex passages smoothly.

MAINTAINING ACCURACY: Maintaining accuracy at high speeds requires ongoing attention and practice. One technique is to practice with "stop and start" methods, where a problematic passage is played up to a challenging note, then stopped and restarted from that point. This technique ensures each transition is smooth and precise. Mental practice, or visualizing the fingerings and movements without playing, can also reinforce accuracy. Regularly recording practice sessions and critically listening to playback can identify areas for improvement.

HAND INDEPENDENCE EXERCISES

SEPARATE HAND PRACTICE: Advanced pianists can benefit from practicing each hand individually to master complex passages and techniques. For instance, focusing on left-hand accompaniments while the right hand remains at rest helps solidify the bass lines and rhythm. Conversely, practicing intricate melodies or fast runs with the right hand while not moving your left hand ensures clarity and precision. This method allows each hand to develop its muscle memory and control without the interference of the other hand, leading to a more balanced and coordinated performance when both hands are combined.

COORDINATION DRILLS: Advanced exercises include polyrhythms, such as playing triplets in one hand against eighth notes in the other or syncopated rhythms that challenge the pianist's hand coordination. Practicing scales and arpeggios in contrary motion (hands moving in opposite directions) or with different articulations (one hand legato, the other staccato) further enhances coordination. These drills train the brain and hands to operate independently yet cohesively.

COMPLEX PIECES: Works by composers like **Bach, Chopin,** and **Rachmaninoff** often involve intricate interplay between the hands. For example, **Bach's** fugues require the pianist to manage multiple voices independently and clearly. At the same time, **Chopin's** etudes often demand contrasting dynamics and articulations between the hands.

IMPROVISATION WITH BOTH HANDS

Advanced pianists can practice improvising with distinct roles for each hand, such as a steady bass line or chordal accompaniment in the left hand and melodic improvisation in the right. Experimenting with different genres, like jazz, blues, or classical, can provide varied challenges and enhance versatility.

PRACTICE TIPS

Practical tips for hand independence include slow and deliberate practice to ensure accuracy and control. A metronome can help maintain consistent timing, mainly when working on polyrhythms or syncopated rhythms. Recording practice sessions allows for critical listening and identification of areas needing improvement. Additionally, incorporating mental practice or visualization techniques can reinforce hand independence by imagining the movements and coordination without physically playing.

My friend **Bo Bice** came very close to winning it all on American Idol. His advice to newcomers is:

"It's not just about waking up and trying to be a star... it's practice, practice, practice. Just practice hard and stay grounded. Treat people like you want to be treated and work hard."

Bo Bice and Tad Sisler
Source – Sisler Private Collection

SECTION TWO
ENHANCING EXPRESSION

I've raised many of the concepts we are discussing in previous chapters. An advanced pianist should double down on exercises to enhance musical expression, moving closer to perfection. Let's bring these concepts home!

CONTROLLING DYNAMICS

Mastery over dynamic range, from pianissimo (very soft) to fortissimo (thunderous), allows for expressive contrasts and subtle gradations in volume. Pianists should practice crescendo (gradually getting louder) and decrescendo (getting progressively softer) exercises, ensuring smooth and controlled transitions. You can achieve this control by varying the weight and speed of the fingers, wrists, and arms. Additionally, understanding the dynamic markings in the score and interpreting them thoughtfully helps create an emotionally engaging performance.

DIFFERENT ARTICULATIONS

Articulation refers to how notes are executed, including staccato (short and detached), legato (smooth and connected), and accents (emphasized notes). Each type of articulation can significantly alter the character of the music. Advanced pianists should practice these articulations in isolation and context, focusing on clarity and precision. For instance, playing a scale legato requires seamless finger transitions, while staccato demands a light, quick touch.

EXPRESSIVE TECHNIQUES

Expressive techniques such as rubato (flexible tempo), pedal usage, and phrasing enhance musical expression. Rubato allows the pianist to alter the tempo to convey emotion and emphasis slightly. At the same time, careful use of the sustain pedal can create resonance and blend sounds harmoniously. Practicing phrasing, or shaping musical sentences, helps deliver the music more naturally and expressively. Pianists should experiment with these techniques, listening critically to how they affect the overall interpretation of the piece. Balancing these elements with dynamics and articulation results in a more compelling performance.

PRACTICE PIECES: Studying works by **Beethoven, Chopin,** and **Debussy** are ideal due to their rich, dynamic contrasts and varied articulations. For instance, returning now and perfecting **Beethoven's** *"Moonlight Sonata"* will help you explore a wide dynamic range and expressive legato phrasing. At the same time, **Chopin's** *"Etudes"* demand precise articulation and nuanced dynamics. Playing **Debussy's** *"Clair De Lune"* with new perspectives offers opportunities to practice subtle dynamic changes and pedal effects.

UNDERSTANDING MUSICAL PHRASES

Musical phrasing is akin to the natural flow of speech, where notes are grouped together to form coherent and expressive musical sentences. For an advanced pianist, understanding musical phrases involves recognizing these segments' start, development, and conclusion within a piece. Phrasing includes identifying cadences, breath points, and dynamic shapes. Practicing phrasing requires attention to the music's overall structure, ensuring that each phrase flows seamlessly into the next. Play with a sense of direction and purpose.

INTERPRETING PIECES

Joanna Hodges always stressed that it is critical to interpret a piece as closely as possible to the perception of how the original composer intended it to be performed. Interpreting a piece involves making artistic decisions about bringing the written score to life. This process includes choices about tempo, dynamics, articulation, and rubato. Advanced pianists should study the score meticulously, considering the composer's indications and the piece's context. Interpretation goes beyond technical execution, requiring a deep emotional connection to the music.

ADDING PERSONAL TOUCH

Adding a personal touch involves infusing personal experiences, emotions, and creativity into the interpretation of the piece. For example, a pianist might emphasize specific phrases differently based on their emotional resonance with the music or add slight timing and dynamics nuances that reflect their artistic vision. This personalization requires a balance between respecting the composer's intent and exploring one's expressive capabilities. The result is an authentic and deeply personal performance that resonates strongly with audiences.

HISTORICAL CONTEXT

Understanding a piece's historical context provides valuable insights into its intended interpretation. Knowing the era, style, and circumstances under which the music was composed can guide pianists in making informed interpretive choices. For instance, the performance practices of Baroque music differ significantly from those of Romantic or Impressionist music, allowing pianists to approach the music with an informed perspective.

ANALYSING FAMOUS PERFORMANCES

Listening to and watching masterful performances provides insights into different interpretive approaches and techniques. By comparing various interpretations of the same piece, pianists can understand how phrasing, dynamics, and expressive nuances can vary while respecting the music's core. Advanced pianists should also critically analyse their performances, recording practice sessions and concerts to identify areas for improvement and new interpretive possibilities.

CONNECTING WITH THE MUSIC

Cultivate a deep emotional connection with the music to enhance your expression. This connection begins with thoroughly understanding the piece's structure, harmony, and thematic elements. By analysing the score and considering the composer's intentions, pianists can uncover the music's emotional core.

EXPRESSING EMOTIONS

Effectively expressing emotions requires more than technical skill; it involves conveying the feelings and moods embedded in the music. Pianists should practice playing passages with different emotional intensities, experimenting with dynamics, tempo, and articulation to find the most compelling expression. This exploration helps identify how best to communicate sorrow, joy, tension, or tranquillity.

STORYTELLING THROUGH MUSIC

Frank Sinatra sang a song as others might speak the lyrics, conveying honesty through his performances. Music has a narrative quality that allows pianists to tell a story through their performance. Advanced pianists can enhance their expressiveness by envisioning the music as a story with a beginning, development, and conclusion. Each phrase and section can represent different characters, emotions, or scenes. Pianists can guide the audience through a journey by crafting a clear narrative arc, making the performance more engaging and memorable.

ENGAGING THE AUDIENCE

Pianists should strive to connect with their listeners, drawing them into the emotional landscape of the music. You can engage through expressive body language, eye contact (when appropriate), and a palpable sense of presence. Before playing, a brief introduction to the piece or sharing personal insights can also enhance audience engagement. The goal is to make the audience feel the emotions conveyed in the music, creating a shared emotional experience that transcends the notes on the page.

PRACTICE EXERCISES

One effective exercise is to play the same passage multiple times, each time focusing on a different emotion (e.g., happiness, sadness, anger, serenity). This exercise helps in exploring the range of expressive possibilities within the music. Another exercise is to practice performing for small, supportive audiences and seek feedback on the emotional impact of the performance. Recording practice sessions and critically listening to them can also reveal areas where expression can be intensified. Additionally, incorporating mindfulness and visualization techniques can help pianists stay emotionally present and focused during practice and performance.

My friend, **President George H. W. Bush**, created a list of motivating thoughts. I turn to this list occasionally, for inspiration to stay emotionally present and focused:

1. Don't get down when your life takes a bad turn. Out of adversity comes challenge and often success.
2. Don't blame others for your setbacks.
3. When things go well, always give credit to others.
4. Don't talk all the time. Listen to your friends and mentors and learn from them.
5. Don't brag about yourself. Let others point out your virtues, your strong points.
6. Give someone else a hand. When a friend is hurting, show that friend you care.
7. Nobody likes an overbearing big shot.
8. As you succeed, be kind to people. Thank those who help you along the way.
9. Don't be afraid to shed a tear when your heart is broken because a friend is hurting.
10. Say your prayers!!"

President George H. W. Bush, Barbara Bush and Tad Sisler
Source – Sisler Private Collection

SECTION THREE
FEEDBACK AND CRITIQUE

In **don Miguel Ruiz's** famous book, **"The Four Agreements,"** the author implores us not to take anything personally, which may be easier said than done. Still, it's a valuable lesson, especially when someone gives you feedback or constructive criticism. Actively seek constructive feedback. Find mentors and participate in masterclasses or workshops conducted by renowned pianists.

ANALYZING FEEDBACK

Engaging in peer reviews is another effective method for obtaining feedback. Fellow musicians, whether from the same level or more advanced, can offer different viewpoints and constructive criticism. Analysing the input received is crucial. Pianists should contemplate all comments with an open mind, discerning which suggestions align with their musical goals and areas needing improvement.

IMPLEMENTING SUGGESTIONS

Implement feedback into practice. You may achieve this by adjusting technical aspects, experimenting with new interpretive choices, or altering practice routines to address specific weaknesses. Documenting the changes made and the outcomes observed helps you track progress and identify what works best.

RECORDING AND REVIEWING

Recording allows pianists to assess their playing objectively from an audience's perspective. Pay attention to accuracy, rhythm, dynamics, phrasing, and overall musicality.

IDENTIFYING STRENGTHS AND WEAKNESSES

Recognizing strengths, such as a strong sense of rhythm or expressive phrasing, is essential for building confidence and reinforcing effective techniques. Conversely, pinpointing weaknesses, such as inconsistent tempo or unclear articulation, provides specific targets for improvement.

SETTING IMPROVEMENT GOALS

Once we identify our strengths and weaknesses, setting specific, measurable, achievable, relevant, and time-bound (SMART) goals can guide improvement efforts. For example, a goal might be improving left-hand accuracy in a piece within two weeks. Analysing practice sessions becomes crucial in this phase. Recording practice sessions, not just final performances, allows for a detailed examination of the learning process. Reviewing these sessions, pianists can see how they tackle difficult passages, manage practice time, and respond to challenges. This self-analysis helps refine practice strategies and maintain motivation.

"Once you replace negative thoughts with positive ones, you'll start having positive results." — Willie Nelson

Willie Nelson
Credit — Wikimedia Commons

HANDLING NEGATIVE FEEDBACK

When receiving criticism, a pianist must remain calm and open-minded, focusing on the content rather than the delivery. Negative feedback can often be emotional and challenging to accept, but it offers valuable insights into areas needing improvement. Pianists should listen carefully, take notes, and avoid becoming defensive. Reflecting on the feedback after some time can help in processing it more objectively.

STAYING POSITIVE

Pianists should remind themselves that criticism is a tool for improvement rather than a personal attack. Embracing a mindset that views challenges as learning opportunities can transform how feedback is perceived. Seeking encouragement and support from mentors, peers, and loved ones can provide a balanced perspective. Positive reinforcement from trusted sources helps bolster confidence and resilience.

EMBRACING A GROWTH MINDSET

Pianists with a growth mindset believe one can develop abilities and intelligence through dedication and hard work. This perspective encourages them to view criticism as a pathway to improvement. They should set specific goals based on the feedback received and devise a plan to achieve them. Regularly revisiting and reassessing progress helps in staying focused and committed to growth. Learning anything requires a mindset, a desire to learn, and a passion to excel. These steps will help you acquire the mindset to achieve mastery and continue evolving throughout your life.

CHAPTER TEN
ACHIEVING MASTERY AND LIFELONG LEARNING

ARTIST SPOTLIGHT
HERBIE HANCOCK

Herbie Hancock is renowned for his extraordinary talent as a legendary jazz pianist and composer, and for his lifelong commitment to learning and evolving his craft. **His career** began in the early 1960s when he joined the **Miles Davis Quintet**, a group that helped to shape modern jazz. During his time with **Davis, Hancock** was exposed to innovative approaches to jazz and constantly pushed the boundaries of traditional jazz forms.

In the 1970s, he embraced electronic instruments and was one of the first jazz musicians to incorporate synthesizers into his work. His groundbreaking album, *Head Hunters*, fused jazz with funk and electronic music, showcasing his willingness to experiment and adapt to new sounds. Throughout his career, **Hancock** never stopped evolving. In the 1980s, he ventured into pop and rock with the hit single *"Rockit,"* which featured turntables and breakdancing, highlighting his openness to different musical influences and his ability to adapt to changing musical landscapes. In the 2000s, **Hancock** continued to innovate, collaborating with artists from diverse genres, including pop, rock, and classical music.

Hancock has been a passionate advocate for music education, serving as the Chairman of the *Herbie Hancock Institute of Jazz*, a role that underscores his commitment to supporting young musicians and promoting jazz education worldwide.

Herbie Hancock
Credit – Wikimedia Commons

SECTION ONE
MASTERY THROUGH CONTINUOUS IMPROVEMENT

Again, it's important to stress the basics, so here I go:

ESTABLISHING A ROUTINE

Consistent practice helps refine techniques, reinforce muscle memory, and develop a deeper understanding of the repertoire. It allows pianists to explore nuances and subtleties in their playing that they can only achieve through repetition and continuous effort. Moreover, daily practice keeps the fingers nimble and the mind sharp, enabling the pianist to perform complex pieces with precision and expressiveness.

OVERCOMING PLATEAUS

Even the most skilled pianists can encounter plateaus where progress seems to stall despite regular practice. Overcoming these plateaus requires advanced practice techniques, such as slow practice to ensure accuracy, practicing hands separately to focus on challenging passages, and using a metronome to maintain rhythm and timing. Incorporating varied practice methods, like playing with different articulations or dynamics, can also break the monotony and stimulate new growth. Pianists push their boundaries and prevent stagnation by setting high goals and embracing challenges, such as tackling complex pieces or learning new styles.

EMBRACING A GROWTH MINDSET

Master pianists often stay motivated by setting achievable goals and celebrating their progress. Embracing a growth mindset is critical; viewing mistakes as learning opportunities rather than setbacks fosters resilience and persistence. Tackling complex pieces and embracing challenges encourages a sense of accomplishment and progression. Learning from errors involves critical self-analysis and seeking constructive feedback, which can guide future practice. This mindset ensures that the pianist remains adaptable and open to new ideas, continuously evolving their craft. My dear friend, iconic actor **Elliott Gould** believed strongly in persistence when he said:

"Quitters don't win, and winners don't quit."

Tad Sisler and Elliott Gould
Source – Sisler Private Collection

I had the honour of working with and performing for **Frank Sinatra**, one of the most iconic vocalists of the 20th century. In addition to being star-struck, I was inspired by knowing that **Mr. Sinatra** achieved mastery through a continuous process of musical evolution and self-improvement. **Sinatra's** career began in the 1930s with the **Harry James** and **Tommy Dorsey** bands, where he honed his craft and developed his distinctive vocal style.

He continuously sought to refine his technique, paying close attention to breath control, phrasing, and emotional delivery. In the 1950s, Sinatra reinvented himself by transitioning from big band music to a solo career, embracing the emerging genre of popular music. He collaborated with renowned arrangers like **Nelson Riddle**, which allowed him to explore complex musical arrangements and innovative recording techniques. Sinatra's commitment to evolving his sound is evident in his timeless albums such as *In the Wee Small Hours* and *Songs for Swingin' Lovers!* He adapted to changing musical landscapes throughout his career, maintaining relevance across different eras. He was so influential that, although he only wrote one song, he is constantly remembered for countless tunes rather than the composers and lyricists who wrote them. In his defence, though, I found him to be extremely generous in crediting composers and musicians during his performances. His meticulous approach to performance, willingness to experiment with new styles, and dedication to perfecting his craft established **Sinatra** as a masterful and enduring figure in music.

Frank Sinatra
Credit - Wikimedia Commons via Picryl.com

SEEKING ADVANCED INSTRUCTION

Finding an experienced and highly qualified teacher specializing in advanced techniques and repertoire can provide personalized guidance and mentorship. These teachers often have extensive performance and teaching experience, offering insights beyond basic instruction. Again, attending workshops and masterclasses is critical for growth.

NETWORKING WITH PEERS

In addition to in-person instruction, online advanced courses have proven to be a valuable resource to learn from esteemed teachers and institutions worldwide. Platforms such as **Coursera, MasterClass,** and the **Juilliard School's** online programs offer advanced courses in piano performance, music theory, and composition. These courses provide flexibility and access to top-tier education from the comfort of one's home.

I WANT TO OFFER YOU A FREE GIFT

I hope you're loving this book so far. Learning an instrument can be daunting, but the rewards are exponential as you learn and grow your performance skills. I've created a list of **TEN SECRETS A MUSICIAN CANNOT LIVE WITHOUT,** and I want to share it with you.

If you want a free copy of my list, email us at...
<<   modernrenaissancepublishing@gmail.com   >>
with the subject line **TEN SECRETS FREE LIST,** and I'll email you back a free copy at no obligation whatsoever to you as a heartfelt thanks for reading this book.

SECTION TWO
LIFELONG LEARNING
KEEPING UP WITH NEW TRENDS

Delving into genres outside your primary expertise, such as jazz, electronic, or world music, can provide fresh perspectives and enhance your musical vocabulary. Adapting to technological advancements is equally essential. Adaptation includes familiarizing yourself with the latest music production software, digital pianos, and recording equipment, enhancing your sound quality, streamlining your workflow, and experimenting with new forms of musical expression.

ARTIFICIAL INTELLIGENCE

AI tools can assist in music composition, provide instant performance feedback, and offer personalized practice routines. Applications like AI-driven music analysis software can help pianists gain deeper insights into their playing and identify areas for improvement. Continuous self-education is vital for staying ahead in the evolving musical landscape. Self-education involves reading the latest research in music theory, pedagogy, and technology and attending seminars, webinars, and conferences. Staying informed about industry developments ensures that pianists can incorporate cutting-edge techniques and knowledge into their practice. Here are some popular AI-powered apps (at the time I'm writing this book) that pianists and keyboardists can use to practice, expand their repertoire, perform, and record:

Yousician provides interactive lessons and real-time feedback for learning piano. It's designed for players of all levels, from beginners to advanced. The app listens to your playing, offering instant pitch, timing, and accuracy feedback, as well as including lessons for various musical skills, such as sight-reading, finger exercises, and playing complete songs. This app is perfect for structured daily practice and learning new pieces step by step.

Flowkey is a piano learning app that provides lessons and interactive sheet music to help pianists learn songs quickly. It listens to your playing and guides you through each piece, focusing on timing and accuracy. It offers different difficulty levels for each song, catering to beginners, intermediate, and advanced players. This app is excellent for expanding repertoire with popular songs, classical pieces, and jazz standards while getting interactive guidance.

Skoove provides AI-driven piano lessons that adapt to your playing. It covers everything from basic scales to advanced pieces, listening to your playing and offering tips to improve your technique. It also teaches music theory concepts alongside practical lessons to give you a deeper understanding of the music you're playing. This app is great for beginners wanting to build a solid foundation in piano or for more experienced players who want to improve specific skills.

Simply Piano by JoyTunes is an AI-powered app designed to help beginners learn piano quickly through step-by-step lessons and popular songs. The app uses real-time feedback to guide learners through exercises. It includes a library of songs for different skill levels and genres. This app is suitable for beginners who want an accessible and engaging way to start learning piano or casual players who wish to practice popular songs.

Moises.ai allows pianists to separate instruments from songs, adjust pitch and tempo, and create custom backing tracks for practice and performance. You can isolate the piano part or other instruments to practice along with or mute them to play the lead. The app also lets you adjust the tempo or pitch of the track to match your level. This app is ideal for pianists who want to practice with backing tracks, learn new songs by isolating piano lines, or prepare for performances.

Playground Sessions is a piano learning app co-created by Quincy Jones. It uses AI-powered lessons to guide pianists through learning songs and techniques. The app provides interactive feedback on your playing, has an extensive library of songs, and includes lessons on music theory and sight-reading. It is suitable for those who want a structured learning path from beginner to advanced, with the ability to track progress.

Piano Marvel uses AI-driven assessment to help pianists improve their skills through detailed feedback on accuracy, rhythm, and dynamics. The app offers interactive lessons, sight-reading exercises, and practice tools that adjust to your skill level. It also provides a scoring system to track your progress. This app suits pianists who want to improve sight-reading, build a solid technique, or track their progress through graded exams.

ScoreCloud is AI-powered music notation software that transcribes your playing into sheet music in real-time. It allows pianists to play a melody or piece, and the app will create sheet music based on what they play. You can edit and print the transcriptions, making it a valuable tool for composition and arrangement. This app is ideal for pianists who compose or improvise and want to transcribe their music into sheet notation quickly.

iReal Pro is a digital practice tool that generates chord charts and backing tracks for various music genres. It provides customizable backing tracks in jazz, pop, rock, and Latin styles, allowing you to practice improvisation or play along with different chord progressions. This app is excellent for jazz pianists who need a practice tool for improvisation or anyone looking to practice with realistic backing tracks.

LANDR is an AI-powered mastering tool that can enhance the quality of your piano recordings. It provides automated mastering, especially for polishing recordings before sharing them online. LANDR also supports music distribution to streaming platforms like Spotify and Apple Music. This tool is excellent for pianists or keyboardists who record their performances and want professional-quality mastering without needing advanced mixing skills.

BENEFITS OF STAYING CURRENT

The benefits of staying current are manifold. It ensures that a master pianist, keyboardist, or studio wizard remains relevant and adaptable in a rapidly changing industry, enhances their teaching and performance skills, and keeps their musical journey exciting and dynamic.

MENTORING AND INSTRUCTION

A master pianist should embrace the role of a music mentor, guiding and inspiring the next generation of musicians. This action involves offering private lessons, conducting masterclasses, and providing personalized feedback to students. By sharing their expertise and experience (like what I'm doing here!), master pianists can help students develop their technical skills, interpretive abilities, and musicality. Additionally, creating instructional content such as online tutorials, video lessons, and written guides allows them to reach a broader audience.

MUSIC EDUCATION PROGRAMS

Participation in music education programs helps cultivate a love for music in diverse communities. It promotes inclusivity and accessibility in music education. Sharing knowledge with peers through collaborative projects, professional associations, and music festivals fosters a vibrant learning environment where ideas and techniques are exchanged.

MUSIC COLLEGES/UNITED STATES:

Schools like the **Musicians Institute** in Hollywood, CA are completely acceptable. **MI** has an excellent vocal, drum, guitar, and audio engineering program. I have friends who work with headliner artists and compose for film and television who have graduated from **MI**. Here are some more prestigious schools of music education:

Juilliard School (New York, NY): **Juilliard** is renowned for its rigorous training and high standards, offering voice and opera performance degrees. Its alumni include **Renee Fleming, Nina Simone, Audra McDonald**, and **David Bryan.**

Berklee College of Music (Boston, MA): Known for its contemporary music programs, **Berklee offers** extensive vocal performance programs, including jazz and popular music. It has a diverse curriculum and notable alumni like **John Mayer** and **Esperanza Spalding**. This program has a high bar for qualification, so you should be excellent and prepared to be the best.

Curtis Institute of Music (Philadelphia, PA): **Curtis** is highly selective, admitting only a few students each year, and provides full-tuition scholarships to all its students. It focuses on classical and opera training with a strong emphasis on performance.

Indiana University Jacobs School of Music (Bloomington, IN): One of the largest music schools in the **United States, Jacobs** offers various programs and degrees in vocal performance. It has a notable faculty and alumni network, including **Joshua Bell** and **Leonard Slatkin.**

New England Conservatory of Music (Boston, MA): **NEC** offers comprehensive programs in voice and opera, with a strong emphasis on performance and musicianship. It is deeply integrated into **Boston's** vibrant music scene.

MUSIC COLLEGES/EUROPE:

Royal College of Music (London, UK): Founded in 1882, this institution is consistently ranked as one of the top music schools globally, offering a wide range of degrees in various musical disciplines and boasting top-notch facilities and a distinguished faculty.

Royal Conservatoire of Scotland (Glasgow, Scotland): Known for its excellent music, drama, and dance programs, the **Royal Conservatoire of Scotland** hosts over 500 public performances each year, providing ample performance opportunities for students.

Royal Academy of Music (London, UK): The oldest conservatoire in the UK, founded in 1822, the **Royal Academy of Music** offers a range of programs from Bachelor's Degrees to advanced diplomas. It has a rich history of producing celebrated musicians such as **Elton John** and **Annie Lennox.**

Conservatoire National Supérieur de Musique et de Danse de Paris (CNSMDP) (Paris, France): Established in 1795, **CNSMDP** is one of **Europe's** leading institutions for music and dance, with comprehensive programs in musical disciplines.

Universität für Musik und darstellende Kunst Wien (Vienna, Austria): Located in **Vienna**, a city renowned for its classical music heritage, this university offers many music degrees. It is one of the largest and most prestigious music schools in **Europe.**

Whatever you do, continually expand your horizons, and never stop learning. My biggest challenge in these times is keeping up with technological advances and staying current. Still, ultimately, making it all boils down to talent and persistence.

SETTING NEW GOALS

This process begins with reflecting on past achievements to understand your strengths and areas for further development. Acknowledging these accomplishments, pianists can identify new challenges that excite and motivate them, such as mastering a new repertoire, composing original works, or exploring innovative performance techniques.

PERSONAL AND PROFESSIONAL BALANCE

While pursuing professional excellence, allocating time for personal interests, family, and self-care prevents burnout and fosters a sustainable career. Music profoundly impacts overall well-being, providing emotional expression, stress relief, and intellectual stimulation. Recognizing this, pianists should set goals to enhance their musical journey and contribute positively to their personal lives. Engaging in any activity promoting physical health, mental relaxation, and emotional fulfillment, such as regular exercise, mindfulness practices, and social interactions, enriches both personal and professional spheres, leading to a more holistic and satisfying life.

ARTIST SPOTLIGHT
ARTHUR RUBINSTEIN

Arthur Rubinstein, legendary 20th century pianist, is a prime example of a lifelong learner who achieved mastery through relentless dedication and passion for music. Despite early struggles and self-doubt in his youth, Rubinstein's unwavering commitment to continuous improvement set him apart. He embraced a rigorous practice regimen and constantly sought new repertoire to expand his horizons. Even at the peak of his career, **Rubinstein** maintained his enthusiasm for learning, often revisiting and reinterpreting pieces with fresh insights. His later recordings, well into his 80s, are celebrated for their profound depth and emotional richness, reflecting a lifetime of growth and refinement. **Rubinstein's** story is a testament to the power of perseverance and the endless learning journey in pursuing artistic excellence.

"At every concert, I leave a lot to the moment. I must have the unexpected, the unforeseen. I want to risk, to dare. I want to be surprised by what comes out. I want to enjoy it more than the audience." — Arthur Rubinstein

Arthur Rubenstein
Credit — Wikimedia Commons

Spontaneity is important in your performances. It keeps the music fresh.

AVOIDING STEREOTYPES

In all my music mastery books, I urge the reader to reject stereotypes. The most important thing you can do is what you don't do! Throughout my life, I've encountered people who bought into the negative stereotypes about musicians. When I mentioned that I was a musician, I would get a look from someone who immediately judged me as a loser. It's sad, but you will do all of us a favor if you exemplify yourself as a professional and never exhibit any of these negative stereotypes. My old friend, championship-winning *NFL* Quarterback, **Congressman and Secretary of Housing & Urban Development Jack Kemp** talked about it in a unique way. He said:

"Winning is like shaving — you do it every day or you wind up looking like a bum."

Tad Sisler and Congressman Jack Kemp
Source — Sisler Private Collection

It's all about the way you carry yourself, with pride and self-respect. People will pick up on your attitudes, emotions, and habits. Be the best version of yourself always and avoid these stereotypes:

MUSICIANS ARE UNRELIABLE AND IRRESPONSIBLE – People often stereotype musicians as flaky, unreliable, and irresponsible, particularly regarding commitments and punctuality. I will immediately write anyone off my call list who can't regularly show up on time with suitable instruments and clothing for the gig.

SUBSTANCE ABUSE – There is a pervasive stereotype that musicians are prone to drug and alcohol abuse, often glamorized in media and popular culture.

FINANCIAL INSTABILITY – Although this is something we cannot always control when we commit to this industry, unfortunately, many people stereotype musicians as struggling financially, living paycheck to paycheck, or unable to support themselves through their music alone. One of my friends who regularly comes to my gig has a running joke with me. He'll say, "You're good. Have you considered doing this for a living?" And I'll say, "No, it doesn't pay enough!" Everyone laughs, but the sad truth is that many musicians are grossly underpaid for their talents. But, don't let this define you.

NO PRACTICAL SKILLS – Musicians are sometimes viewed as lacking practical or marketable skills outside of their music, contributing to the idea that they have few career options.

EGO AND ARROGANCE – Musicians, especially successful ones, are often stereotyped as having big egos or arrogant, believing they are superior because of their talent. I've worked with many excellent musicians who were impossible to work with. We sounded great on stage together, but the whole experience was not worth it because of their egos or negativity. Always try to enjoy the experience and let go!

UNCONVENTIONAL LIFESTYLE – There is a stereotype that musicians lead unconventional or chaotic lifestyles with irregular hours, frequent travel, and unstable relationships.

EMOTIONAL INSTABILITY – People sometimes judge as emotionally unstable or overly sensitive, with intense mood swings or dramatic behaviour.

PROMISCUITY – Particularly in rock and pop culture, musicians are often stereotyped as promiscuous and engaging in numerous short-term relationships. Groupies don't help erase this stereotype!

NON-CONFORMITY – People often see musicians as rebels or non-conformists who reject societal norms and conventional careers.

LACK OF FORMAL EDUCATION – There's a stereotype that musicians are less formally educated or lack academic achievements, focusing solely on their craft.

These stereotypes are not universally true and can be harmful, as they overlook many musicians' diversity, dedication, and professionalism. I must admit, though, that I've often told people I'm a composer, producer, author, entertainer, or many other titles (all true) besides musician. Help propel us all forward by going against the stereotype!

SECTION THREE
THE JOY OF MASTERY
CELEBRATING MILESTONES

Acknowledging progress, whether mastering a challenging piece, completing a significant project, or achieving a professional goal, provides motivation and a sense of accomplishment. Hosting recitals and performances is a meaningful way to celebrate these milestones. Pianists can showcase their progress to an audience by organizing concerts and gaining validation and appreciation for their hard work.

SHARING YOUR JOURNEY

Recording progress through audio or video documentation is another effective way to celebrate milestones. Keeping a record of performances and practice sessions allows pianists to reflect on their growth over time, providing a tangible measure of their achievements. Sharing this journey with others through social media, blogs, or personal websites helps build a supportive community of followers and fellow musicians who can offer encouragement and feedback.

MAKE IT A LIFELONG PASSION

Music as a lifelong passion offers profound therapeutic benefits, providing a source of solace, relaxation, and mental well-being. Playing music daily can serve as a form of meditation, reducing stress and anxiety while fostering a sense of inner peace. The repetitive and rhythmic nature of practice can be soothing and invigorating, helping musicians find joy in their daily routines. Beyond the technical aspects, music becomes a powerful means of self-expression, allowing individuals to convey emotions and stories that might be difficult to articulate with words. This emotional connection to music enriches life, making each practice session a meaningful and rewarding experience. Remember the words of the great pianist **Lang Lang:**

" When you play, make sure your fingers are connected to your heart. It's ok to be controlled by your brain – but to really enjoy the music, you have to go directly from your fingers to your heart. "

Lang Lang
Credit – Wikimedia Commons

BUILD A LEGACY

Embracing music as a lifelong passion enables musicians to contribute to their communities' cultural and artistic tapestry through their performances, compositions, and teaching. Sharing their journey and wisdom with aspiring musicians inspires the next generation to pursue their musical dreams. Whether through formal education or informal mentoring, seasoned musicians can pass down their knowledge and passion, fostering a continuous cycle of growth and creativity. Nurturing young talent ensures that the art of music remains vibrant and evolving, creating a legacy that transcends time and touches countless lives.

FINAL THOUGHTS AND ENCOURAGEMENT

Congratulations on starting your journey with *"Mastering the Piano and Keyboards: The Complete Guide with Exercises and Music Theory for All Skill*

Levels." As you continue exploring and developing your musical abilities, remember that the path to mastery is as much about the journey as the destination. Believe in your potential and trust that every practice session, every challenge, and every note you play brings you one step closer to your goals. Your dedication and passion for music are your greatest assets, and they will guide you through your musical journey.

> *"To play a wrong note is insignificant; to play without passion is inexcusable." – Vladimir Horowitz*

Embrace the journey with an open heart and mind. Stay committed to your practice, and don't be afraid to make mistakes—they are opportunities for growth and learning. Find inspiration in every note, whether playing a simple exercise or a complex composition. Let the music speak to and through you, and allow it to be a source of joy, comfort, and expression. Remember that learning and mastering the piano and keyboards is a lifelong adventure filled with endless possibilities and discoveries.

Stay curious, stay passionate, and always remember why you fell in love with music in the first place. Every musician has a unique voice, and your journey is uniquely yours. Celebrate your progress, no matter how small, and keep pushing yourself to new heights. You have the potential to create beautiful music that is inspiring and touching to others. Keep playing, keep dreaming, and let your love for music guide you every step of the way.

> *"Keep searching for that sound in your head until it becomes a reality." – Bill Evans*

CONCLUSION

RECAP OF KEY POINTS: In this book, we embarked on an enriching journey of musical discovery and growth. From choosing the right instrument and setting up an ideal practice space to mastering basic techniques and delving into advanced musical theory, this guide has covered a comprehensive range of topics. We've explored the importance of structured practice routines, the benefits of understanding music theory, and the joy of expanding your repertoire across various genres. Each chapter aims to provide practical advice, exercises, and motivational insights to help you become a proficient and expressive pianist or keyboardist. Remember the importance of persistence, practice, and passion. Challenges and plateaus are a natural part of learning but also opportunities for growth. Stay committed to your practice, embrace the difficulties, and celebrate your achievements, no matter how small they may seem. Finding inspiration in every note and enjoying the learning process will keep your passion for music alive. Believe in your potential and trust that every effort you put into your practice brings you closer to mastering your instrument.

Now that you've equipped yourself with the knowledge and tools from this book, it's time to act. Set new goals, challenge yourself with new pieces, and never stop learning. Whether mastering a complex composition, performing in front of an audience, or simply enjoying the therapeutic benefits of playing music, continue to push your boundaries and grow as a musician. Share your progress and stories with others, inspire fellow musicians, and build a community that fosters mutual growth and support.

FINAL NOTE: Thank you for embarking on this journey with *"Piano and Keyboard Mastery."* Your dedication and passion for music are commendable. I hope this guide has been a valuable resource in your pursuit of musical excellence. Remember, mastering an instrument is a lifelong adventure filled with endless possibilities. Keep playing, keep learning, and most importantly, find joy in every moment you spend with your piano or keyboard. Your story and progress can inspire others. Don't hesitate to share your musical experiences and continue spreading your love for music.

SUMMARY: I have drawn from a lifetime of experience to create a comprehensive guide for learning to play piano and keyboards. Each chapter includes hooks and segues for smooth transitions, focusing on a passion for performance, technique, and personal desires and incorporating mindfulness and motivational tips throughout. The structure covers all aspects of learning, from basic techniques to advanced practice, ensuring readers find value at every skill level. I designed this book with case studies, anecdotes, and practical advice to inspire you on your unique journey to an extraordinary life as a master musician.

PLEASE LEAVE A REVIEW

Now that you have everything you need to **excel in playing piano**, it's time to share your newfound knowledge and show other readers where they can find the same guidance.

Simply by leaving your honest opinion of this book on Amazon or wherever you purchased it, you'll help other **pianists and keyboardists** discover the information they're looking for and pass their passion for **playing music** forward.

Thank you for your help. The **passion for playing piano** is kept alive when we pass on our knowledge — and you're helping **me** to do just that.
If you purchased my book on Amazon, here's the link to leave your review:

https://www.amazon.com/review/review-your-purchases/?asin=196625802X

Or you can just scan this QR code to get to the Amazon review page:

Thanks!!!!

ABOUT THE AUTHOR

Tad Sisler is an American Composer, Author and Producer of feature films and music. More than a thousand of his original works are available through *iTunes, Amazon* and virtually every other major marketplace. Through the years, **Tad** created and released independent feature films and documentaries, television shows, developed a music store and vast collection of music for film and television usages, in addition to published screenplays and books. **Tad** is a voting member of *The Academy of Recording Arts & Sciences.* **Tad** invented a wireless karaoke all-in-one microphone that became a best-seller on *Amazon.* A child prodigy, Tad was playing advanced piano pieces at the age of 8, and rating superior in Classical piano competitions at 12. Tad won his first scholarship for singing at 12, attending the Idyllwild School of Music and the Arts, then affiliated with the University of Southern California.

FEATURE FILMS
Tad produced, edited, and released "**The Ghosts of Brewer Town**", a mystery feature film, currently available on *YouTube.*
TELEVISION PROJECTS
Tad launched the **Journey To An Extraordinary Life-Legends Among Us** documentary series, which chronicles the lives and careers of legendary artists, actors, sports figures and heroes of medicine, in a feature-film format.
BOOKS
Books, Audio Books and Podcasts released by **Tad** include "**Reflections in the Key of Life-The Steve Madaio Story**", chronicling the life and times of America's most prolific trumpeter. This book garnered a **Readers' Favorite Book Award** for Tad.
"**Mafia Baby**" is a shocking true story of a woman raped by a Mafioso, who then raised his child alone. Tad's autobiography, "**It's a Long Climb to The Middle**" *is* available currently on *Amazon* and *Barnes & Noble.* Screenplays in development by Tad Sisler include "**The Incredible Spark of Franklin Benjamin**", and "**Please Don't Forget**". **Tad's** latest **Music Mastery** collection of books is designed to educate and inspire musicians to become masters.
MUSIC
Tad's production music catalog tripled in size with the addition of thousands of excellent production music tracks, as well as hundreds of sound-alike tracks for the DJ/Karaoke industry, now distributed on **iTunes, Amazon Marketplace, CD Baby, Spotify, Rdio, Xbox Music** and dozens of other outlets Worldwide. **Tad** produced and released "The Barcelona Sessions" to 1000 radio stations Worldwide, with never- before-heard original performances by Miles Davis' bassist, Bill Evan's drummer, Frank Sinatra's saxophonist, Maynard Ferguson's guitarist, and Andrae Crouch' flutist/saxophonist, produced by Tad Sisler in his recording studio.

Tad Sisler composed the full score to "**The Encore Of Tony Duran**", an indie feature film starring **Elliott Gould, William Katt, Nicki Ziering and Cody Kasch**, along with his co- composer Andrew Fraga, Jr.

After having the distinction of being the first film to sell-out at the prestigious *Palm Springs International Film Festival*, the film won the **Jury Award** for **Best Feature Film** at the *Las Vegas Film Festival* and the *Santa Fe Film Festival*, as well as the **Indie Spirit Award** at the *Fort Lauderdale Film Festival* and the **Audience Favorite Award** at *Tallgrass Film Festival*, in conjunction with a **Lifetime Achievement Award** for **Elliott Gould**. The film is available on *Amazon Prime*.

Tad completed the music and audio editing for the TV Series "**American M.C.**". The first 7 episodes are complete and in the process of distribution through **iTunes**. Tad scored the Main Title theme to **American M.C.** as well as underscore and providing Music Supervision and source music.

PRODUCTION

Tad Sisler has been a valuable member of the team of specialists and project developers for **Yamaha Corporation of America**, delivering hundreds of intricate projects to exact **Yamaha** specifications over a 10 year period.

Tad received accolades in 2011 after being given the honor and challenge of doing the "official" remake of the iconic "**Andy Griffith Theme**" for the estate of the composer **Earle Hagen** as a perfect sound-alike, along with his composing associate Andrew Fraga, Jr.

Following a stint composing for a series entitled "**Famous Families**" on **Foxstar** and working as assistant to composer Jeff Edwards on the television series "**Silk Stalkings**" and "**Renegade**" in the late 1990's, Tad Sisler founded & developed a production music catalog, containing thousands of high-quality music tracks available for sync licenses in film, television and advertising in more than 150 genres.

In addition to handling Music Supervision on "**The Encore Of Tony Duran**", and on "**American M.C.**", "**The Ghosts of Brewer Town**", "**Tis' The Season**", the "**Journey To an Extraordinary Life**" series, **Tad** produced the "**It's Everyone Else Who Has A Problem!**" series, and placed his original music on **NBC, ABC/Disney, Warner Brothers Television, TNT**, US National Infomercial campaigns through **Guthy/Renker** and **Script To Screen**, as well as custom composing for the TV and Advertising industry. **Tad** released contains hundreds of top-quality soundalike tracks produced by **Tad** and his associates, for DJ and Karaoke usages, currently on *ITunes, Amazon Marketplace, Spotify, Rdio, Xbox Music*, and many other outlets.

LIVE PRODUCTION

In the 1980's and 1990's, **Tad** and his team produced a series of live headliner events at multiple venues from the ground up, including sold-out performances by **Kenny Rogers, Earth, Wind & Fire, Los Lobos, Glen Campbell, The Righteous Brothers, Lou Rawls, Tito Puente,** the **Power Jam** featuring **Timmy T, Tara Kemp, Candyman, Soul To Soul** and more.

HISTORY

As a very young man, Tad Sisler worked as a performer for **Frank Sinatra**, studied music in choreography under world-famous Broadway Dancer/Choreographer **Jacque D'Amboise**, received superior ratings in classical piano performance in tough **Joanna Hodges** international competitions, and received private acting lessons from **Richard Burton**, a friend of his family.

Tad attended the prestigious **Idyllwild School of Music and the Arts** on vocal music scholarships during the period when it was affiliated with the **University of Southern California**. In High School, Tad was one of 100 statewide vocalists elected to the prestigious **All-State Choir** in Missouri.

During his storied career, Tad has also had the honor of performing with and working among such greats as **Gladys Knight, Rita Coolidge, B.B. King, Marilyn McCoo, Johnny Mathis, Kenny Rogers, Tito Puente, Sonny and Mary Bono, Gene Barry, Teri Cole Whittaker, Shecky Greene, Peter Marshall, Mary Hart, Blackwell, Herb Jeffries, Trini Lopez, Glen Campbell, Jennifer Hudson** and other legends.

Tad Sisler's extensive experience, state of the art facility and history of delivering quality feature films and music on time and on budget, as well as the ability to draw from an extensive catalog of production music, allows his experienced team to offer complete services in custom film and television production as well as in music composition and production efficiently.

Tad is proud and humbled to be a voting member of the **Academy of Recording Arts & Sciences**, which allows him to have a voice to vote for great artists worthy of winning a **Grammy Award**. Many of Tad's works have been placed into Grammy consideration.

In 2023, Tad won a prestigious **Telly Award** for creative excellence in his *Journey to an Extraordinary Life* film series.

Modern Renaissance Publishing is at the forefront of a new intellectual awakening, dedicated to fostering a renaissance of ideas that resonate in today's world. Our mission is to bring cutting-edge concepts and timeless wisdom to the public through a diverse array of publishing formats, including books, eBooks, and audiobooks.

We are proud to launch our **Music Mastery** series, offering comprehensive guides and insights for musicians of all levels. In addition to our literary endeavors, we also publish original music, enriching the cultural landscape with creative expressions.

Whether you're seeking to expand your knowledge, enhance your skills, or simply be inspired, **Modern Renaissance Publishing** provides the resources and content to empower your journey. Join us as we bridge the rich heritage of the past with the innovative spirit of the present to shape a brighter, more enlightened future.

REFERENCES

License link to all Wikimedia Commons and Creative Commons photo credit references: Creative Commons. (n.d.). *Attribution-ShareAlike 4.0 International (CC BY-SA 4.0)* [License]. Retrieved from
https://creativecommons.org/licenses/by-sa/4.0/ **https://creativecommons.org/licenses/by-sa/3.0/**
Goodreads. (n.d.). *I used to be disgusted; now I'm just amused.* Retrieved November 5, 2024, from
https://www.goodreads.com/quotes/51784-i-used-to-be-disgusted-now-i-m-just-amused
TalkClassical. (2019). *A Bach quote.* Talk Classical. Retrieved from **https://www.talkclassical.com/threads/a-bach-quote.62091/**
Yamaha. (n.d.). *Keyboards.* Yamaha. Retrieved from
https://usa.yamaha.com/products/musical_instruments/keyboards/index.html
Roland. (n.d.). *Keyboards.* Roland. Retrieved from **https://www.roland.com/us/categories/keyboards/**
Sweetwater. (n.d.). *Musical instruments and pro audio.* Sweetwater. Retrieved from **https://www.sweetwater.com/**
Piano Buyer. (n.d.). *Piano Buyer - The Definitive Guide to Buying New, Used, and Restored Pianos.* Piano Buyer. Retrieved from **https://www.pianobuyer.com/**
Piano Technicians Guild. (n.d.). *Home.* PTG. Retrieved from **https://www.ptg.org/home**
TakeLessons. (n.d.). *15 Beautiful Quotes Every Piano Player Will Love.* TakeLessons. Retrieved from
https://takelessons.com/blog/15-beautiful-quotes-every-piano-player-will-love
Pianist Magazine. (n.d.). *Home.* Pianist Magazine. Retrieved from **https://www.pianistmagazine.com/**
Soundproof Cow. (n.d.). *Soundproof Cow: Expert Soundproofing & Acoustic Panels.* Soundproof Cow. Retrieved from **https://www.soundproofcow.com/**
MusicNotes. (n.d.). *25 Quotes from Musicians for Musicians.* MusicNotes. Retrieved from
https://www.musicnotes.com/blog/25-quotes-from-musicians-for-musicians/?utm_source=google&utm_medium=cpc&utm_campaign=PMax%3A%20%28ROI%29%20Smart%20Shopping%20-%20High%20Converters&utm_id=17863025684&utm_content=&utm_term=&gad_source=1&gclid=CjwKCAjw4ri0BhAvEiwA8oo6F3z_nu0PoQ-dhR64xR-leWbVjlX-xOaf4AvpoofEDZpf_2ieRPY1fBoCd0oQAvD_BwE
MusicTheory.net. (n.d.). *Music theory lessons, exercises, and tools.* Retrieved from **https://www.musictheory.net**
BrainyQuote. (n.d.). *Rod Stewart quotes.* BrainyQuote. Retrieved from
https://www.brainyquote.com/authors/rod-stewart-quotes
BrainyQuote. (n.d.). *Pianist quotes.* BrainyQuote. Retrieved from **https://www.brainyquote.com/topics/pianist-quotes**
BrainyQuote. (n.d.). *Trini Lopez quotes.* BrainyQuote. Retrieved from
https://www.brainyquote.com/authors/trini-lopez-quotes
BrainyQuote. (n.d.). *Glen Campbell quotes.* BrainyQuote. Retrieved from
https://www.brainyquote.com/search_results?x=0&y=0&q=glen+campbell
BrainyQuote. (n.d.). *Melodies quotes.* BrainyQuote. Retrieved from
https://www.brainyquote.com/search_results?x=0&y=0&q=melodies
BrainyQuote. (n.d.). *Larry King quotes.* BrainyQuote. Retrieved from
https://www.brainyquote.com/search_results?q=larry+king&pg=3
BrainyQuote. (n.d.). *Kenny Rogers quotes.* BrainyQuote. Retrieved from
https://www.brainyquote.com/search_results?q=kenny+rogers

BrainyQuote. (n.d.). *Billy Joel quotes*. BrainyQuote. Retrieved from
https://www.brainyquote.com/search_results?x=0&y=0&q=BILLY+JOEL
BrainyQuote. (n.d.). *Bill Medley quotes*. BrainyQuote. Retrieved from
https://www.brainyquote.com/search_results?x=0&y=0&q=bill+medley
BrainyQuote. (n.d.). *Coordination quotes*. BrainyQuote. Retrieved from
https://www.brainyquote.com/search_results?x=0&y=0&q=coordination
YouTube. (n.d.). *Video of a drummer performance*. Retrieved from
https://www.youtube.com/watch?v=xV6A0zl0VPo
Paper Adepts. (n.d.). *Trevor Hoffman quotes*. Paper Adepts. Retrieved from
https://www.paperadepts.com/quotes/authors/trevor_hoffman/7/
BrainyQuote. (n.d.). *Improvisation quotes*. BrainyQuote. Retrieved from
https://www.brainyquote.com/search_results?x=0&y=0&q=IMPROVISATION
BrainyQuote. (n.d.). *Gerald Ford quotes*. BrainyQuote. Retrieved from
https://www.brainyquote.com/search_results?q=GERALD+FORD&pg=2
BrainyQuote. (n.d.). *Robert Wagner quotes*. BrainyQuote. Retrieved from
https://www.brainyquote.com/search_results?q=robert+wagner
BrainyQuote. (n.d.). *Counterpoint quotes*. BrainyQuote. Retrieved from
https://www.brainyquote.com/search_results?x=0&y=0&q=counterpoint
BrainyQuote. (n.d.). *Composing quotes*. BrainyQuote. Retrieved from
https://www.brainyquote.com/search_results?q=composing&pg=6
BrainyQuote. (n.d.). *Junior Seau quotes*. BrainyQuote. Retrieved from
https://www.brainyquote.com/search_results?q=junior+seau&pg=2
BrainyQuote. (n.d.). *Fusion quotes*. BrainyQuote. Retrieved from
https://www.brainyquote.com/search_results?x=0&y=0&q=FUSION BrainyQuote. (n.d.). *Bruce Hornsby quotes*. BrainyQuote. Retrieved from
https://www.brainyquote.com/search_results?x=0&y=0&q=BRUCE+HORNSBY
Ray Charles. (n.d.). *Home*. Ray Charles Official Website. Retrieved from **https://raycharles.com/**
BrainyQuote. (n.d.). *Fear quotes*. BrainyQuote. Retrieved from
https://www.brainyquote.com/search_results?q=fear&pg=2
BrainyQuote. (n.d.). *Lorenzo Lamas quotes*. BrainyQuote. Retrieved from
https://www.brainyquote.com/search_results?x=0&y=0&q=LORENZO+LAMAS
BrainyQuote. (n.d.). *Overcoming quotes*. BrainyQuote. Retrieved from
https://www.brainyquote.com/search_results?x=0&y=0&q=overcoming&pg=2
BrainyQuote. (n.d.). *Mary Tyler Moore quotes*. BrainyQuote. Retrieved from
https://www.brainyquote.com/search_results?x=0&y=0&q=mary+tyler+moore
BrainyQuote. (n.d.). *Dyan Cannon quotes*. BrainyQuote. Retrieved from
https://www.brainyquote.com/search_results?x=0&y=0&q=DYAN+CANNON
IMDb. (n.d.). *Dyan Cannon quotes*. IMDb. Retrieved from **https://m.imdb.com/name/nm0058001/quotes/**
BrainyQuote. (n.d.). *Fulfillment quotes*. BrainyQuote. Retrieved from
https://www.brainyquote.com/search_results?x=0&y=0&q=fulfillment
BrainyQuote. (n.d.). *Piano practice quotes*. BrainyQuote. Retrieved from
https://www.brainyquote.com/search_results?x=0&y=0&q=PIANO+PRACTICE
BrainyQuote. (n.d.). *Bo Bice quotes*. BrainyQuote. Retrieved from
https://www.brainyquote.com/search_results?x=0&y=0&q=BO+BICE
Goodreads. (n.d.). *George H.W. Bush quotes*. Goodreads. Retrieved from
https://www.goodreads.com/author/quotes/579816.George_H_W_Bush
Ruiz, M. (n.d.). *The Four Agreements*. MiguelRuiz.com. Retrieved from **https://www.miguelruiz.com/the-four-agreements**
Herbie Hancock. (n.d.). *Home*. Herbie Hancock Official Website. Retrieved from
https://www.herbiehancock.com/
Sinatra, F. (n.d.). *Home*. Sinatra.com. Retrieved from **https://www.sinatra.com/**
Love, T. (2018). SMART Goals. *Advancing Diverse Healthcare Executives, 33*(6), 58-60.
Soukoreff, R. W., & MacKenzie, I. S. (1995). Theoretical upper and lower bounds on typing speed using a stylus and a soft keyboard. *Behaviour & Information Technology.* **https://doi.org/10.1080/01449299508914656**
Akkords.ru. (n.d.). *Уроки игры на гитаре / Транспонировка аккордов*. Akkords.ru. Retrieved from
https://www.akkords.ru/lessons/transp.php
Sadiya, A., Abdi, S., & Abusnana, S. (2016). Lifestyle Intervention for Weight Loss: A group-based program for Emiratis in Ajman, United Arab Emirates. *Diabetes, Metabolic Syndrome and Obesity, 9*, 101-108.
BrainyQuote. (n.d.). *Quotes by musicians*. BrainyQuote. Retrieved from
https://www.brainyquote.com/profession/quotes-by-musicians

BrainyQuote. (n.d.). *Diana Krall quotes.* BrainyQuote. Retrieved from
https://www.brainyquote.com/authors/diana-krall-quotes
Grimaud, H. (n.d.). *Helene Grimaud quotes.* AZQuotes. Retrieved from
https://www.azquotes.com/author/84839-Helene_Grimaud#google_vignette
BrainyQuote. (n.d.). *Tori Amos quotes.* BrainyQuote. Retrieved from
https://www.brainyquote.com/search_results?x=0&y=0&q=tori+amos
Goodreads. (n.d.). *Persistence quotes.* Goodreads. Retrieved from https://www.goodreads.com/quotes/2749-
nothing-in-this-world-can-take-the-place-of-persistence
YouTube. (2023). *[Journey To an Extraordinary Life-Tad Sisler and Louie Stevens].* YouTube.
https://www.youtube.com/watch?v=-wYCSRDyIic
ScienceDaily. (2024, January 29). *Playing an instrument boosts brain's executive function, study finds.* ScienceDaily.
https://www.sciencedaily.com/releases/2024/01/240129122415.htm
Cross-Eyed Pianist. (2024, March 18). *10 inspirational & thought-provoking quotes from musicians and composers.*
The Cross-Eyed Pianist. https://crosseyedpianist.com/2024/03/18/10-inspirational-thought-provoking-
quotes-from-musicians-and-composers/
Pianist Magazine. (n.d.). *10 iconic pieces of piano advice from 10 pianists.* Pianist Magazine.
https://www.pianistmagazine.com/blogs/10-iconic-pieces-of-piano-advice-from-10-pianists/
Golden Key Piano School. (n.d.). *Resonant wisdom: Timeless quotes from piano virtuosos.* Golden Key Piano
School. https://goldenkeypianoschool.com/resonant-wisdom-timeless-quotes-from-piano-virtuosos/
AZ Quotes. (n.d.). *Elliott Gould quotes.* AZ Quotes. https://www.azquotes.com/author/31289-Elliott_Gould
QuoteFancy. (n.d.). *Norman Vincent Peale quotes.* QuoteFancy.
https://quotefancy.com/quote/877976/Norman-Vincent-Peale-There-is-only-one-group-of-people-who-do-
not-have-problems-and-they

MODERN RENAISSANCE
PUBLISHING

www.ingramcontent.com/pod-product-compliance
Lightning Source LLC
Chambersburg PA
CBHW060935120626
46557CB00003B/1005